A Seven-Fold Promise Of His Soon Coming

Dan Goodwin

Bill Waugh

Dan Goodwin

117 E. 18th St. #165

Owensboro, KY 42303

270-363-6336

www.godsfinaljubilee.com

Daniel@godsfinaljubilee.com

A Seven-fold Promise of His Soon Coming

ISBN: 978-1-60208-143-7

First Printing March 2008

5,500 Copies

Revised – 2015

July 2015 – 1,000

Printed in the United States of America by
FBC Publications & Printing
Fort Pierce, FL 34982
www.fbcpublications.com

Table of Contents

"Looking for that blessed hope, and the glorious appearing of the great God and our Saviour Jesus Christ;" Titus 2:13

Introduction

This is not just another book dealing with prophecy. This may be the most up to date and timely book on prophetic events of our day! Dan Goodwin and Bill Waugh believe that some end time mysteries can be seen today like never before and that some hidden prophetic truths of Daniel have been UNSEALED in these last days! You will not be able to put this book down until you have read every chapter! Learn why we believe we are somewhere near the two-thousandth year of God's time clock. Discover the truth about the New Testament beginning not at the birth of Christ, but at Calvary. Christmas has blinded us for centuries! You will get a look at the seven major feasts and why the Feast of Trumpets would make a great day for the rapture. See how a Jewish man got his bride in the Old Testament, and how it is not only a beautiful picture of Christ coming for His espoused Bride, but sheds light on prophetic truth as well. Get solid Biblical proof of a pre-tribulation rapture. Learn why we believe there will be 6000 years of human history and then a 1000-year Sabbath rest. This is a book to stir up the slumbering Christian and revive the defeated Saint, as well as encourage and bring hope to the working but exhausted laborer of God!

The surest fact in the world is not death, but the return of the Lord Jesus Christ!

~ M. R. DeHaan (1947)

Daniel's 70th Week

Chapter One

Daniel 9:22-27

Daniel 9:22 And he informed me, and talked with me, and said, O Daniel, I am now come forth to give thee skill and understanding.

23 At the beginning of thy supplications the commandment came forth, and I am come to shew thee; for thou art greatly beloved: therefore understand the matter, and consider the vision.

24 Seventy weeks are determined upon thy people and upon thy holy city, to finish the transgression, and to make an end of sins, and to make reconciliation for iniquity, and to bring in everlasting righteousness, and to seal up the vision and prophecy, and to anoint the most Holy.

25 Know therefore and understand, that from the going forth of the commandment to restore and to build Jerusalem unto the Messiah the Prince shall be seven weeks, and threescore and two weeks: the street shall be built again, and the wall, even in troublous times.

26 And after threescore and two weeks shall Messiah be cut off, but not for himself: and the people of the prince that shall come shall destroy the city and the sanctuary; and the end thereof shall be with a flood, and unto the end of the war desolations are determined.

27 And he shall confirm the covenant with many for one week: and in the midst of the week he shall cause the sacrifice and the oblation to cease, and for the overspreading of abominations he shall make it desolate, even until the consummation, and that determined shall be poured upon the desolate.

An understanding of Daniel's 70th week in this passage will help you greatly in grasping the timeline of end time events. Daniel Chapter 9 is probably the most important chapter in the entire Bible concerning the end times! Let us give you a brief study of it here by just making some observations from the passage.

1. The theme of the passage is the 70 weeks.

2. These "weeks" are literally weeks of years as we see from the context.

Each week represents seven years. 70 weeks would equal 490 years in all. Remember that Jacob worked seven years for each of his wives, and the Bible says in Genesis 29:27 "*fulfill her week,*" speaking of a seven-year period of time.

3. These weeks are concerning Israel, not the Church.

In verse 24, we see that "*Seventy weeks are determined upon thy people and upon thy holy city,*" and of course, the people are the Jews, and the holy city is Jerusalem. We need to get this settled right from the beginning. The Church is not going to be here for this seven-year period called the Tribulation. It has nothing to do with us. It is for Israel.

4. The purpose of these 70 weeks is given in verse 24.

1) To finish the transgression

2) To make an end of sins

3) To make reconciliation

4) To bring in everlasting righteousness

5) To seal up the vision

6) To anoint the most Holy

Have you ever asked yourself why there needs to be the Seven-year Tribulation? It is to put an end to sin, bring reconciliation, bring to fulfillment God's prophecy, bring in righteousness, anoint the Lord Jesus Christ as King of Kings and Lord of Lord's, and begin the reign of Christ during the 1000-year Millennium. It is also about redeeming the earth. Man's spirit is redeemed at salvation. Our body will be redeemed at the rapture, the main harvest. The earth will be redeemed during the Tribulation when the Seven Sealed Book, the title deed to the earth, is opened.

5. 69 of the 70 weeks have already been fulfilled.

In verses 24-26 of our passage, we see this is true. Briefly, the first seven weeks (49 years) took place in Ezra and Nehemiah at the building of the temple and the walls around the city. Then the next 62 weeks (434 years) take place from Nehemiah's wall until Christ is "cut off" at Calvary. This leaves 1 week (7 years) yet to be fulfilled after all believers are taken out of here.

6. Daniel's 70th week is yet to come.

God's time clock stopped for Israel when Christ was "cut off" and crucified at Calvary. One of the reasons we are so confused about the dating of the calendar today is because we have started the New Testament at the birth of Christ, instead of at Calvary. We will deal more with that later. For the last 2000 years, we have been in the Church Age. When we get to Revelation Chapter 4, all the saved will be raptured, and God's time clock will begin again with the final week of seven years we call Daniel's 70th week. The Church Age will be over. Look again at Daniel 9:25-26 and you will see that from the time the command came to restore and to build Jerusalem, (483 years before Calvary) until it was completed, even in times of trouble and danger, was 7 weeks (49 years). Then another 62 weeks (434 years) until Messiah is "cut off" to pay the sin debt of the world. Have you ever wondered why the people were waiting for the Messiah to ride into Jerusalem on what many call Palm Sunday? It is because of this timeline; they knew right to the day when Messiah was to arrive, 483 years after the command to build the wall. Check Ussher's dates back in Ezra and Nehemiah and add 33 years until Calvary and it comes out to around 483 years. That is why we read that many of the women in Joseph and Mary's day were hoping to be the chosen one, and many prophesied of His soon appearing. They did not know the month or day He would be born, but they knew right to the day when the Messiah would enter the city.

7. **This 70th week (Seven-year Tribulation) yet to come begins at the rapture in Revelation Chapter 4 and is in two 3 1/2 year periods.**

See Daniel 9:27 and understand that in the "midst" or middle of the week of seven years, the Antichrist shall enter the temple. (This temple will be built before or right after the rapture on the temple mount. In fact, it may be built for the Jews by Antichrist himself.) As the Antichrist enters the temple, he will end the sacrifices, declare he is God, and break the peace treaty with Israel. Matthew 24:15-24 gives reference to what Daniel spoke of and calls it the "Great Tribulation." II Thessalonians 2:4 shows the defiling of the temple at the middle of the Tribulation. Revelation 13:5-6 also speaks of this time.

See below:

Matthew 24:15-24 When ye therefore shall see the abomination of desolation, spoken of by Daniel the prophet, stand in the holy place, (whoso readeth, let him understand:) Then let them which be in Judaea flee into the mountains: Let him which is on the housetop not come down to take any thing out of his house: Neither let him which is in the field return back to take his clothes. And woe unto them that are with child, and to them that give suck in those days! But pray ye that your flight be not in the winter, neither on the sabbath day: For then shall be great tribulation, such as was not since the beginning of the world to this time, no, nor ever shall be. And except those days should be shortened, there should no flesh be saved: but for the elect's sake those days shall be shortened. Then if any man shall say unto you, Lo, here is Christ, or there; believe it not. For there shall arise false Christs, and false prophets, and shall shew great signs and wonders; insomuch that, if it were possible, they shall deceive the very elect.

2 Thessalonians 2:4 Who opposeth and exalteth himself above all that is called God, or that is worshipped; so that he as God sitteth in the temple of God, shewing himself that he is God.

Revelation 13:5-6 And there was given unto him a mouth

speaking great things and blasphemies; and power was given unto him to continue forty and two months. And he opened his mouth in blasphemy against God, to blaspheme his name, and his tabernacle, and them that dwell in heaven.

Let us summarize what we learned so far:

1. **The rapture is imminent; it could happen anytime.**

It is the next event on God's calendar. It could happen today. Are you ready?

2. The saved will not go through the Tribulation, but instead will be raptured.

1 Thessalonians 5:9 *For God hath not appointed us to wrath, but to obtain salvation by our Lord Jesus Christ....*

Revelation 3:10 *Because thou hast kept the word of my patience, I also will keep thee from the hour of temptation, which shall come upon all the world, to try them that dwell upon the earth.*

Notice, He promised to save them FROM the hour, not after the hour, or in the midst of the hour. Read again Daniel 9:24 and see that the Tribulation has nothing to do with us.

3. The rapture is that "blessed hope" we await.

Titus 2:13 "*Looking for that blessed hope, and the glorious appearing of the great God and our Saviour Jesus Christ; . . .*" It would not be a blessed hope if it were at the end.

Pre-Tribulation Rapture

Chapter Two

Before we get into too much depth concerning the translation of all believers from the earth, it is important that we get a firm grasp on when the Bible says this translation, or rapture as we call it, is going to occur. We strongly believe the Bible teaches a pre-tribulation rapture. In other words, the rapture of all believers will take place right before the Seven-year Tribulation.

1 Thessalonians 4:13-18 But I would not have you to be ignorant, brethren, concerning them which are asleep, that ye sorrow not, even as others which have no hope. For if we believe that Jesus died and rose again, even so them also which sleep in Jesus will God bring with him. For this we say unto you by the word of the Lord, that we which are alive and remain unto the coming of the Lord shall not prevent them which are asleep. For the Lord himself shall descend from heaven with a shout, with the voice of the archangel, and with the trump of God: and the dead in Christ shall rise first: Then we which are alive and remain shall be caught up together with them in the clouds, to meet the Lord in the air: and so shall we ever be with the Lord. Wherefore comfort one another with these words. Two other passages for the rapture are: I Corinthians 15:42-56 and John 14:1-4

The Bible teaches that all believers will be taken out of this world to meet the Lord in the air at the rapture. This takes place right before the Seven-year Tribulation, which is also called Daniel's 70th week. (Daniel 9:24) The word "rapture" is not in the Bible but comes from the words "caught up" in our text. There are three views concerning when the rapture will occur. The pre-tribulation view is that the rapture occurs before the Tribulation. The mid-tribulation view is that the rapture occurs at the middle of the seven years, and the post-tribulation view is that it occurs at the end and that all believers will go through the terrible Tribulation. We shall not take the time debating the errors of the latter two, but rather, let us look at some reasons why we believe the rapture comes before the Seven-year Tribulation:

1. **Because the rapture is imminent**

In other words, it could happen any moment! If the rapture is to happen in the middle or at the end, it would be easy to pinpoint the rapture to the very day, and would not be a surprise, thus it would not be imminent.

See the following Scriptures:

Luke 12:40 Be ye therefore ready also: for the Son of man cometh at an hour when ye think not.

Matthew 24:36 But of that day and hour knoweth no man, no, not the angels of heaven, but my Father only.

Matthew 25:13 Watch therefore, for ye know neither the day nor the hour wherein the Son of man cometh.

2. Because the rapture is the "blessed hope"

Titus 2:13 Looking for that blessed hope, and the glorious appearing of the great God and our Saviour Jesus Christ;

What is blessed is that Christ comes and delivers us from the Tribulation to come upon the world. This would not be considered the "blessed hope" at the middle or the end of the Tribulation. Praise the Lord!

3. Because the Lord has not appointed believers to wrath

The Tribulation is the wrath of God upon this world as well as God dealing with Israel. God has not appointed the saved to wrath. (Do not confuse chastisement and persecution that believers go through with God's wrath, they are two separate things entirely.)

1 Thessalonians 5:9 For God hath not appointed us to wrath, but to obtain salvation by our Lord Jesus Christ,

Romans 8:1 There is therefore now no condemnation to them which are in Christ Jesus, who walk not after the flesh, but after the Spirit.

John 5:24 Verily, verily, I say unto you, He that heareth my word, and believeth on him that sent me, hath everlasting life, and shall not come into condemnation; but is passed from death unto life.

Revelation 3:10 Because thou hast kept the word of my patience, I also will keep thee from the hour of temptation, which shall come upon all the world, to try them that dwell upon the earth.

See also Daniel 9:24-27

4. Because there is no mention of the church after Revelation Chapter 4

The seven churches are mentioned in Chapter 2 and 3 of Revelation, the Rapture takes place in Revelation Chapter 4:1 followed by the seven years of the Tribulation. The reason the church is not mentioned again until the end is because all believers have been taken out at the rapture, and God is dealing again with the Jews in the 70th week mentioned in Daniel 9:27. The Tribulation is Old Testament.

5. Because of the removal of the Restrainer, The Holy Spirit of God, who indwells all believers

The Antichrist comes on the scene as the first horseman at the BEGINNING of the Seven-year Tribulation in Revelation Chapter 6.

Revelation 6:1-2 And I saw when the Lamb opened one of the seals, and I heard, as it were the noise of thunder, one of the four beasts saying, Come and see. And I saw, and behold a white horse: and he that sat on him had a bow; and a crown was given unto him: and he went forth conquering, and to conquer.

This is speaking of the Antichrist, who comes on the scene at the beginning of the Seven-year Tribulation. (Do not confuse him with Jesus who comes on a white horse in Revelation 19:11) The Bible teaches us that this Antichrist, this man of sin, does not show up until after all believers are taken away. Look carefully at 2 Thessalonians 2:1-8.

1 Now we beseech you, brethren, by the coming of our Lord Jesus Christ, and by our gathering together unto him,

2 That ye be not soon shaken in mind, or be troubled,

neither by spirit, nor by word, nor by letter as from us, as that the day of Christ is at hand.

3 Let no man deceive you by any means: for that day shall not come, except there come a falling away first, and that man of sin be revealed, the son of perdition;

4 Who opposeth and exalteth himself above all that is called God, or that is worshipped; so that he as God sitteth in the temple of God, shewing himself that he is God.

5 Remember ye not, that, when I was yet with you, I told you these things?

6 And now ye know what withholdeth that he might be revealed in his time.

7 For the mystery of iniquity doth already work: only he who now letteth will let, until he be taken out of the way.

8 And then shall that Wicked be revealed, whom the Lord shall consume with the spirit of his mouth, and shall destroy with the brightness of his coming:

Notice in verse 2 that "the day of Christ" is the second coming of Christ at the end of the Seven-year Tribulation. Then we see clearly in Revelation 6 that the Antichrist arrives on the scene on a white horse when the first seal is opened at the beginning of the Tribulation.

It is plain that the Scriptures teach a pre-tribulation rapture. The Holy Spirit cannot leave without us my friend, as He indwells all believers. We believe the reference is to all believers and the Holy Spirit's influence and restraining power leaving. All the "salt and light" will be gone.

Note: As America gets further from God, and as God's

people get more worldly, we see less restraining power of God and more activity that is demonic.

Imagine a whole world with no Christians and no Holy Spirit restraint! America is getting more wicked every day. Just take a moment and think of all the demonic television programs that we have given into.

6. **Because of the Old Testament types of the rapture**

    1) Enoch was removed from God's wrath BEFORE the floods came.

    2) Lot was delivered from Sodom BEFORE the fire fell.

    3) Noah was lifted up above the floodwaters.

7. **Because of the Twenty-four Elders in the book of Revelation**

From Revelation 4:4 to 19:4 they are mentioned twelve times. We believe these Elders represent all believers in Heaven after the Rapture. Just look at the characteristics of these Elders and it is plain: The crowns they cast at His feet, their praise of God, their clothing, etc. As soon as the trumpet sounds in Chapter 4:1, all believers are assembled in Heaven represented by the Twenty-four Elders.

8. **Because of the contrast between the rapture and the second coming**

The two simply **cannot** be at the same time, or be the same event. See just a few examples below:

Rapture	2nd Coming
Coming for us John 14:1-4 1 Thess. 4:14-17	Coming with us Rev. 19:14, Jude 1:14
As a thief in the night 1 Thess. 5:2	Every eye shall see Him Rev. 1:7
Meets us in the clouds 1 Thess. 4:16-17	Coming on a white horse Rev. 19:11
Imminent 1 Thess. 5:4-6 Luke 12:40	At end of 7 years 2 Thess. 2:3-8

9. The Church cannot be overcome by Satan, but the Tribulation saints will be.

(Matthew 16:18) *And I say also unto thee, That thou art Peter, and upon this rock I will build my church; and the gates of hell shall not prevail against it.*

(Revelation 13:7) *And it was given unto him to make war with the saints, and to overcome them: and power was given him over all kindreds, and tongues, and nations.*

If the saints in Revelation 13 can be overcome by Satan, they are not the church.

The next great event on God's prophetic calendar is the rapture. Are you certain that you are saved? Only saved folks will go to Heaven when the trump of God sounds. If you are saved, will you be ashamed of the life you lived when you meet Him in the air? Are you living like you expect He could come today? Do you have friends and loved ones that are not ready to meet the Lord?

Someone came up with a nice acrostic we want to share with you:

P- Placement of the church in Revelation

R- Removal of restraining power

E- Exempt from God's wrath

T- Twenty-four Elders

R- Rapture contrasted with Second Coming

I- Imminent return of Christ

B- Blessed hope

A Wedding Made in Heaven

Chapter Three

Revelation 21:2 And I John saw the holy city, new Jerusalem, coming down from God out of heaven, prepared as a bride adorned for her husband.

Revelation 21:9 And there came unto me one of the seven angels which had the seven vials full of the seven last plagues, and talked with me, saying, Come hither, I will shew thee the bride, the Lamb's wife.

In the last chapter, we looked at nine reasons why all believers are translated, or taken in the rapture, just before the Seven-year Tribulation. In our text above, we see that all believers are going to be the Bride of Christ when He comes for us. At the rapture, for the first time ever, all believers will be a church assembled in perfect unity without spot or blemish and will become the Bride of Christ. Another verse on the subject is *John 3:29 He that hath the bride is the bridegroom: but the friend of the bridegroom, which standeth and heareth him, rejoiceth greatly because of the bridegroom's voice: this my joy therefore is fulfilled.*

In this chapter, we are going to look at the Jewish practice of betrothal and marriage and see how it typifies Christ coming for His Bride at the rapture. It is a shame how little understanding that most of us have of Jewish customs and practices. Did you know that many of the parables and stories Jesus gave cannot be fully understood without understanding Bible customs? Many of the parables and truths that Jesus taught were intertwined around the Jewish customs of that day. Most of the Scriptures that deal with Christ coming for His Bride coincide perfectly with the Jewish customs of a man taking a bride. As you will see, an understanding of these customs is the key to a better understanding of the truths concerning the rapture and of our becoming the Bride of Christ.

The following is a systematic process of how a Jewish man got his bride in Bible days. We want you to see how it coincides with Bible prophecy, and we trust that its truths will forever reinforce your beliefs concerning the things that are to shortly come to pass!

How a Man Got a Bride in Bible Days

A Type of Christ and His church

1. The man would make his offer to purchase his bride.

We see this in the story of Rebekah in Genesis 24. This would be with the permission of her father of course, and there may or may not have been some courting. He could even be a complete stranger to her, as in the case of Isaac and Rebekah. The woman could only be his bride if she consented willingly, and the groom paid a price for her.

You and I were also purchased at a great price: Acts 20:28 *"...the church of God, which he hath purchased with his own blood."* However, He does not force us to be His Bride; we must choose to accept Him and His payment.

Some similarities of Rebekah and a person trusting Christ:

- **a.** She trusted a person she had never seen, just as you and I must trust a Saviour we have only heard about through the Scriptures.
- **b.** She received a free gift. Our salvation is a free gift from God. Romans 6:23 "... *but the gift of God is eternal life through Jesus Christ our Lord.*
- **c.** She left her kingdom for his kingdom.
- **d.** It was an act of her own free will. "Whosoever will."

2. Next, a marriage contract is given.

This contract spells out the conditions, inheritance, and obligations of the marriage. (Jacob had a contract for both his wives.)

This would be like the vows that a husband makes at the altar that shows that even some of our traditions are rooted in Jewish custom. Just as the groom gives the bride a contract, Jesus has given us His Word, the Bible, a covenant, filled with His promises to us, His Bride.

John 14:1-3 *Let not your heart be troubled: ye believe in God, believe also in me. In my Father's house are many mansions: if it were not so, I would have told you. I go to prepare a place for you and if I go and prepare a place for you, I will come again, and receive you unto myself; that where I am, there ye may be also.*

3. **When the bride accepts and receives the purchase price, she is formally betrothed.**

The actual ceremony may not take place for months, and there is no physical contact until the ceremony. (Story of Joseph and Mary) Betrothed means contracted for future marriage. Espoused means promised in marriage by contract. She will continue to live with her parents until he returns for her. When you and I accept the gift of eternal life, we are saved and become the purchased property of Christ immediately, but we have no physical contact, just like Jewish custom. We are espoused to Christ, but are not actually the bride until He comes for us at the rapture. 2 Corinthians 11:22 *For I am jealous over you with godly jealousy: for I have espoused you to one husband, that I may present you as a chaste virgin to Christ.*

4. **The Groom then goes back to his father's house to prepare for his new bride.**

(Prepares a bridal chamber)

a. He leaves the purchase price with her, a kind of guarantee. We get the Holy Spirit as a down payment, as a surety that He is coming back for us. Ephesians 1:14 *Which is the earnest of our inheritance until the redemption of the purchased possession, unto the praise of his glory.*

b. He may be gone for quite a while. Our Saviour has been gone for nearly 2000 years now!

c. He promises to return for her. The bride is to watch and wait.

John 14:2-3 "*...I go to prepare a place for you. And if I go and prepare a place for you, I will come again, and receive you unto myself; that where I am, there ye may be also.*"

This passage will mean more to you now than ever before! Jesus has gone back to Heaven, to the Father's house. He is preparing a place for His Bride. As soon as it is ready, He is coming back for us! That is the rapture, the end of the Church Age.

5. The bride-to-be was to prepare herself for his sudden return.

a. It is in her marriage contract to do so. Our marriage contract is the Bible. We are to be growing in grace and preparing for His return. She was to purify herself, and keep herself for only him. 2 Corinthians 11:2 *For I am jealous over you with godly jealousy: for I have espoused you to one husband, that I may* *present you as a chaste virgin to Christ.*

b. She was to be ready and waiting to go with him at any moment! She was to have her bags packed and be ready to go at a moment's notice. We too are to be ready at any moment for the coming of Christ. This is more proof that the rapture is before the Tribulation, and that it could happen any moment. Luke 12:40 *Be ye therefore ready also: for the Son of man cometh at an hour when ye think not.*

Revelation 19:7 *Let us be glad and rejoice, and give honour to him: for the marriage of the Lamb is come, and his wife hath made herself ready.*

If we would only believe that we are the espoused bride of Christ, it would affect the way that we live. The truth is, most of us are unfaithful, and most of God's people do not even faithfully read the Word of God, His love letter to us.

6. The bride-to-be would participate in a ritual of being immersed.

What a symbol of baptism...a new convert gets baptized after salvation. Not only does that get the believer into the church, but it is also a beautiful picture of what our Groom did to purchase us.

7. Only the father of the groom knows the date of the marriage.

Neither the woman nor the groom knows the date of the wedding, as the father decides when the house is ready. Truth is, if it were up to us men, we would just elope and live in a shack!

Matthew 24:36 *But of that day and hour knoweth no man, no, not the angels of heaven, but my Father only.*

8. **The woman would light an oil lamp for the groom each night.**

This is symbolic of her expecting and hoping he would come that night. It also helped the groom find her window at night, as well as let other men know she was espoused. Hey, does this world's crowd know that you belong to the King of Kings? Oil is also symbolic of the Holy Ghost. The light symbolizes Jesus, the light of the world. Now you will better understand the parable of the ten virgins in Matthew 25 next time you read it.

9. **When the father decides that it is time, he sends the groom to get the bride and prepares for the ceremony.**
   a. This announcement was made to the son with the sounding of trumpets. 1 Corinthians 15:51-57, 1 Thessalonians 4:16 and Revelation 4:1 all speak of the rapture occurring with a trumpet.

   b. Guests are invited to the wedding.

   c. A shout was made at the door…this was the signal for the bride to rush out to meet him, as well as a normal propriety for modesty sake. The groom would meet her at the door and carry her out. (This may be where we got the tradition of carrying the bride over the threshold) Hey, at the rapture we are caught up! It is very possible, in light of this, that the trumpet is heard only in heaven.

d. This was usually done at night and in secret.

Christ is coming for us *as a thief in the night*.

e. The lost world does not even know you left to get married.

10. The wedding ceremony takes place.

At the wedding would be the Rabbi, the Best man, two witnesses, and friends. The two witnesses may be the Father and the Holy Ghost. The Rabbi would be the Word of God, and the friends would be the Old Testament people.

11. The couple enters the bridal chamber and has a seven-day honeymoon.

This symbolizes the seven years we are in Heaven during the Tribulation. What a contrast! The Judgment Seat takes place here, where the Groom brags on the good of His Bride. Jesus will reward His Bride and brag on her before all of Heaven.

12. At the end of the seven-day honeymoon, the couple goes to their new home.

This would be the time of the marriage supper as well. We would call it a reception today, and it would take place after the wedding, but not in Bible times.

Application:

1. Am I espoused to Christ?
2. Am I faithful to Him?
3. Am I daily making myself ready to meet Him?
4. Am I inviting others to the wedding?
5. Do I expect His coming tonight?
6. Is my lamp shining brightly?

We trust that a deeper understanding of these Jewish customs will help open up the prophetic truths of the Scriptures and that you will strive to be faithful to Jesus Christ.

"Jesus began His ministry with a wedding (John 2) and He will end His ministry with a wedding when He comes for His Bride."

— Dan Goodwin

Signs of the Times

Chapter Four

(Matthew 16:3) And in the morning, It will be foul weather to day: for the sky is red and lowring. O ye hypocrites, ye can discern the face of the sky; but can ye not discern the signs of the times?

Are we living in the last days? Let us start out by saying that the Bible teaches that we have been in the last days since Christ rose from the dead. Look at what it says in *Hebrews 1:2 Hath in* ***these last days*** *spoken unto us by his Son, whom he hath appointed heir of all things, by whom also he made the worlds;* See, since Jesus came, God says we have been in "the last days". Look at *Acts 2:17 And it shall come to pass* ***in the last days****, saith God, I will pour out of my Spirit upon all flesh: and your sons and your daughters shall prophesy, and your young men shall see visions, and your old men shall dream dreams:* This actually was prophesied in Joel 2:28-32 and most of this was fulfilled in Acts 2 on the day of Pentecost, as Peter says.

Notice that this Scripture along with Joel 2 is speaking of the last days which started during the New Testament Age. Nevertheless, we believe the Bible also speaks of the last days in another sense. We believe that God speaks of the drawing nigh of the second coming of Christ, which is preceded by the rapture and the Seven-year Tribulation, as the last days. We call it "The Last of the Last days." Look with us at what the Bible says in *2 Peter 3:3-4 Knowing this first, that there shall come in the last days scoffers, walking after their own lusts, And saying, Where is the promise of his coming? for since the fathers fell asleep, all things continue as they were from the beginning of the creation.*

Did you notice that while Peter is writing some years AFTER the resurrection, he speaks of some terrible events that SHALL COME in the last days? Obviously a future event he is speaking of, the last of the last days, the time that we believe you and I are living in right now. You might want to look up Isaiah 2:2 and Micah 4:1 for more reference to the last days. Let us give you another important passage that we think will shed more light on the subject:

2 Timothy 3:1-5 *This know also, that in the last days perilous times shall come. For men shall be lovers of their own selves, covetous, boasters, proud, blasphemers, disobedient to parents, unthankful, unholy, Without natural affection, trucebreakers, false accusers, incontinent, fierce, despisers of those that are good, Traitors, heady, highminded, lovers of pleasures more than lovers of God; Having a form of godliness, but denying the power thereof: from such turn away.*

Did you notice that Paul makes the same point that Peter did? Paul said that "perilous times shall come," speaking of a FUTURE event. Paul, while living in the last days, the New Testament Age, says that in the future, in the last days, these signs will be prevalent. Are you with us so far? We have been in the LAST DAYS since Jesus, but the

Bible speaks of the last of the last days, the time right before the rapture, the days that lead up to the coming of Christ. Now that we have made that clear, let us give you some reasons we strongly believe we are in the last of the last days.

1. Because of the signs given in 2 Timothy 1: 1-5

Look back at the Scripture above, and notice the signs he gave of how things would be in the last days: *"Lovers of their own selves,"* me, my, mine. Does that sound like us? *"Covetous,"* keeping up with the Jones's? Got to have what the neighbor has; *"boasters, braggers, proud, blasphemers, disobedient to parents,"* the streets are full of them. "*Unthankful, unholy, without natural affection*," my friend, how is it that millions of babies have been aborted? Consider the small amount of time that parents spend with their children today, with their work schedules, daycare, selfish divorces, etc. "*Trucebreakers*," my friend, a man's word use to mean something, but not so today. "*False accusers, incontinent, fierce, despisers of those that are good, traitors, heady, highminded, lovers of pleasures more than lovers of God";* my friend, the lakes and pools and movie houses are full on Sunday, while the church is near empty. "*Having a form of godliness*," this is our religious crowd. They have the talk, but they are ungodly. My friend, the signs of the times point to the soon returning of Christ.

2. Because of the increased ease and use of travel of our generation

Daniel 12:4 *But thou, O Daniel, shut up the words, and seal the book, even to the time of the end: many shall <u>run to and</u>*

fro, and knowledge shall be increased.

Many shall "run to and fro" is a sign given of the time of the end.

3. The tremendous and almost frightening increase and availability of knowledge.

Daniel 12:4 *But thou, O Daniel, shut up the words, and seal the book, even to the time of the end: many shall run to and fro, and knowledge shall be increased.* It is amazing when you think how fast the access of knowledge is since √the computer came about. In addition, every year they are smarter, faster, and easier to use. These are signs the Word of God is giving us of what it will be like in the last days before Christ returns.

4. Lack of faith is a sign of the end.

Look what Jesus said concerning the time of His return in Luke 18:8. *I tell you that he will avenge them speedily. Nevertheless when the Son of man cometh, shall he find faith on the earth?*

The average person does not even know how to define faith, let alone live by faith. Let me give you my definition of faith from Hebrews Chapter 11. Faith is believing that God will do what He said in the Bible He will do. Apart from the truths in the Bible, a person cannot even practice faith. We see our generation trusting in Government, not God, in money not prayer, in insurance rather than Scripture. Now I am not against these things, I am just saying that we are not to put our trust in them.

5. The fact that the average born again child of God does not believe He is coming soon, is itself possibly one of the greatest signs of all that He is soon coming back and we are in fact living in the last days.

Luke 12:40 Be ye therefore ready also: for the Son of man cometh at an hour when ye think not.

The Church is fast asleep! Christ's coming is drawing near, but the average Christian is eating, drinking, and being merry as they did in Noah's day. We know, the Bible says, "*No man knoweth the day or the hour*", but the Bible says in *1 Thessalonians 5:1 But of the times and the seasons, brethren, ye have no need that I write unto you. 2 For yourselves know perfectly that the day of the Lord so cometh as a thief in the night. 3 For when they shall say, Peace and safety; then sudden destruction cometh upon them, as travail upon a woman with child; and they shall not escape. 4 But ye, brethren, are not in darkness, that that day should overtake you as a thief. 5 Ye are all the children of light, and the children of the day: we are not of the night, nor of darkness. 6 Therefore let us not sleep, as do others; but let us watch and be sober.*

My friend, we may not know the exact day or month or year, but God has given us signs. Verse 4 tells us we are not in darkness, and the day of Christ's coming does not have to catch us off guard.

Let us look for His coming, let us live holy lives, let us win everyone to Christ that we can before it is too late. He told us to "*Watch and be sober*". Let us live as if we expect He may come back for us today!

6. Because in our generation, for the first time in history, one man can effectively rule the whole world.

Through the technology of computers, satellite, phones, and the high speed of travel, one man could actually rule the whole world. The Antichrist will rule the world after we are gone. Never before has a generation been able to understand prophecy, the mark of the beast, and world destruction like our generation can. Daniel 12:9 *And he said, Go thy way, Daniel: for the words are closed up and sealed till the time of the end.*

7. Because of the developments in Israel in our generation

Preachers that know Bible prophecy will tell you to "keep your eyes on Israel." You see, the end-times (tribulation) are all about Israel, not the Church. Let us give you some facts about Israel that are signs of Christ's soon return:

a. Israel was recognized by the world as a nation in 1948. Do you understand that no other nation in the history of the world that had ceased to exist has ever recovered their statehood? None except one that is, Israel. The U.N. gave the land of Israel to the Jews in 1948, however, Israel got Jerusalem in 1967 after the miraculous Six-Day War. We lean towards 1967 as "*The fig tree buddeth.*" What is Israel without Jerusalem?

b. The anointing oil needed to anoint the high priest, as well as Jesus, has been discovered after nearly 2000 years. The tree that this oil comes from has been extinct for years. In 70 A.D.

when Jerusalem was destroyed, some flasks of this oil were hidden under ground and were just discovered in recent years.

c. We have read that they now have the "red heifer" needed for the sacrifice.

d. Everything needed for rebuilding the temple is ready. Many more things could be mentioned, but understand that Israel is more ready for the events of the Tribulation than ever before in history! Read Matthew 24 and you will see that the temple must be ready right after the rapture. As we said earlier, it is possible that the Antichrist will in fact build the temple for them after they sign the seven-year peace treaty.

e. Because of the dam on the Euphrates River

The Bible speaks of the Euphrates River drying up and the kings of the east crossing to invade Israel. This would be China. Right now, there is a dam already in place that can stop the river from flowing, making way for the "Kings of the East." Revelation 16:12 *And the sixth angel poured out his vial upon the great river Euphrates; and the water thereof was dried up, that the way of the kings of the east might be prepared.*

8. Because we live in the generation that for the first time in history has the power to destroy itself.

Mark 13:20 makes it clear that at the final battle at the end of the seven years, that the nations would have destroyed themselves unless Christ had come.

And except that the Lord had shortened those days, no flesh should be saved: but for the elect's sake, whom he hath chosen, he hath shortened the days.

Military people say that Russia right now has 10,000 ICBM's aimed at the United States of America. Each one of these intercontinental ballistic missiles is more powerful than the bombs dropped on Japan! From the time the button is pushed, it only takes about 15 minutes to reach its target here in America. Can you imagine if even half of them make it through? America would cease to exist! Many small heathen nations around the world have nuclear weapons. Recently, North Korea announced that it has nukes. It would not take much for a worldwide nuclear war to break out. Iran is very close to having the bomb. America has bombs that are so powerful that they have not even been tested! Notice in the first four seals of Revelation 6 that one-fourth of the world's population will die as a result of war. That is around 1 billion souls! In the first half of the Tribulation, half the world's population will die and go to an eternity in hell. Never before has a generation understood this prophecy as we can. George Washington, with his black powder musket, certainly could not understand it as we can. The world is more unstable today than it has ever been in history. The financial markets, oil, nukes, terrorism, over crowded prisons, sodomy, greed and lust are trademarks of the last days. You and I had better get ready for the return of the Lord!

9. Because of the description given of the last church on earth before the trumpet sounds.

We are speaking of the Laodicean Church in Revelation 3:14-18.

And unto the angel of the church of the Laodiceans

write; These things saith the Amen, the faithful and true witness, the beginning of the creation of God; I know thy works, that thou art neither cold nor hot: I would thou wert cold or hot. So then because thou art lukewarm, and neither cold nor hot, I will spue thee out of my mouth. Because thou sayest, I am rich, and increased with goods, and have need of nothing; and knowest not that thou art wretched, and miserable, and poor, and blind, and naked: I counsel thee to buy of me gold tried in the fire, that thou mayest be rich; and white raiment, that thou mayest be clothed, and that the shame of thy nakedness do not appear; and anoint thine eyes with eyesalve, that thou mayest see.

This is a description of the average church on earth at the rapture. Does its wall to wall carpeting, big screen monitors, and look at us attitude seem too familiar? Look at the description of this church:

Lukewarm, wretched, miserable, poor, blind, naked, this is a type of the church that shall be in existence at the rapture and it clearly fits the characteristics of most churches and believers today. You see, all Scripture has three interpretations, the literal, the figurative, and the prophetic. These seven churches in Revelation 2 and 3 are literal churches that existed in John's day. They also teach many types and lessons for us today. However, in light of Revelation being a prophetic book, the main teaching for us is a prophetic one. These seven churches are prophetic of seven periods of the 2000-year Church Age. The Laodicean Church is prophetic of the last church of the Church Age that probably started around the year 1901. When you turn the page to Revelation 4:1, we see the rapture take place, and no more mention of the church until after the Second

Coming of Christ in Revelation 19:11.

After this I looked, and, behold, a door was opened in heaven: and the first voice which I heard was as it were of a trumpet talking with me; which said, Come up hither, and I will shew thee things which must be hereafter.

Revelation 4:1

10. Because the whole world seems to be groaning in want and expectation of some catastrophic event.

Romans 8:22 For we know that the whole creation groaneth and travaileth in pain together until now.

Matthew 24:3-8 And as he sat upon the mount of Olives, the disciples came unto him privately, saying, Tell us, when shall these things be? and what shall be the sign of thy coming, and of the end of the world? And Jesus answered and said unto them, Take heed that no man deceive you. For many shall come in my name, saying, I am Christ; and shall deceive many. And ye shall hear of wars and rumours of wars: see that ye be not troubled: for all these things must come to pass, but the end is not yet. For nation shall rise against nation, and kingdom against kingdom: and there shall be famines, and pestilences, and earthquakes, in divers places. All these are the beginning of sorrows.

In the Olivet discourse in Matthew 24, the things mentioned in verses 5-8 appear to be warning signs, or you could say, tremors leading up to the big quake. *So likewise ye, when ye shall see all these things, know that it is near, even at the doors.* Matthew 24:33

Just think of the tremendous increase in natural disasters in just the last few years alone. Doesn't it just feel like something is about to happen? Something big?

In closing this chapter, let us give you one more important fact that shows we are very near the end of this age. We believe there are going to be 7000 years of history down here. This will be discussed in more detail later, but consider the following: God's special number is seven. It is the number of perfection and completeness. There are seven notes in a scale, seven colors in the rainbow. It is God's number. There are seven churches in Revelation, seven trumpets, seven seals, etc. There are seven days of creation. Those seven days are prophetic of 7000 years of history. There are seven major feasts for Israel, and something big happened on each of those feast days. Christ died on Feast of Passover; lay in the grave on Feast of Unleavened Bread, and He rose on Feast of Firstfruits. The Church was empowered on Feast of Pentecost. These four feasts look back at what has taken place. The next three feasts look forward. Feast of Trumpets is a type of the rapture. Many believe Christ will come on the Feast of Trumpets. It certainly would be the day we would choose if we were God. Then the Feast of Day of Atonement, Yom Kippur, a perfect time for the second coming of Christ, and followed by Feast of Tabernacles, a type of the Millennium, God's rest. The seven days of creation are a type of seven thousand years of the world.

2 Peter 3:8 *But, beloved, be not ignorant of this one thing, that one day is with the Lord as a thousand years, and a thousand years as one day.*

Compare that with Hosea 6:2 *After two days will he revive us: in the third day he will raise us up, and we shall live in his sight.* This is speaking of God dealing with the Jews after the 2000 year Church Age!

Psalm 90:4 *For a thousand years in thy sight are but as yesterday when it is past, and as a watch in the night.* Interesting, this Psalm was written by Moses who will be one of the two witnesses during the first half of the Tribulation.

These verses clearly hint at a 7000-year period of history down here on the earth! If that is true, and we need the last 1000 years for the millennial reign, then we are just about at the end! We are right now on the verge of the 6000th year. If we are very close to the end of the 6000th year of history, don't you think God will have His Sabbath rest? Do you really think that God will put it off for a few years? He punished Israel for not remembering the Sabbath; we do not believe He will be late.

This is no time to be backslidden! Get your heart right with the Lord today! Decide to start doing more for God than you ever have before. Live your life as if He may come today. There is too much prophecy in the Bible to ignore it. God told Daniel to ". . .*seal up the book till the time of the end.*"

The Creative Week

Chapter Five

Genesis 1:1 In the beginning God created the heaven and the earth.

God created in six days, and rested on the seventh. We believe that these seven days of creation in Genesis 1 are prophetic of 7000 years of human history on the earth. We believe each of the days of creation represent a thousand years. We believe 6000 years will pass, and God will rest, and the Millennium will be ushered in. We also believe we are very close to the end of that 6000th year. Read the following passage and pay close attention to verse eight:

2 Peter 3:1-18 *This second epistle, beloved, I now write unto you; in both which I stir up your pure minds by way of remembrance:*

2 That ye may be mindful of the words which were spoken before by the holy prophets, and of the commandment of us the apostles of the Lord and Saviour:

3 Knowing this first, that there shall come in the last days scoffers, walking after their own lusts,

4 And saying, Where is the promise of his coming? for since the fathers fell asleep, all things continue as they were from the beginning of the creation.

5 For this they willingly are ignorant of, that by the word of God the heavens were of old, and the earth standing out of the water and in the water:

6 Whereby the world that then was, being overflowed with water, perished:

7 But the heavens and the earth, which are now, by the same word are kept in store, reserved unto fire against the day of judgment and perdition of ungodly men.

8 But, beloved, be not ignorant of this one thing, that one day is with the Lord as a thousand years, and a thousand years as one day.

9 The Lord is not slack concerning his promise, as some men count slackness; but is longsuffering to us-ward, not willing that any should perish, but that all should come to repentance.

10 But the day of the Lord will come as a thief in the night; in the which the heavens shall pass away with a great noise, and the elements shall melt with fervent heat, the earth also and the works that are therein shall be burned up.

11 Seeing then that all these things shall be dissolved, what manner of persons ought ye to be in all holy conversation and godliness,

12 Looking for and hasting unto the coming of the day of God, wherein the heavens being on fire shall be dissolved, and the elements shall melt with fervent heat?

13 Nevertheless we, according to his promise, look for new heavens and a new earth, wherein dwelleth righteousness.

14 Wherefore, beloved, seeing that ye look for such things, be diligent that ye may be found of him in peace, without spot, and blameless.

15 And account that the longsuffering of our Lord is salvation; even as our beloved brother Paul also according to the wisdom given unto him hath written unto you;

16 As also in all his epistles, speaking in them of these things; in which are some things hard to be understood, which they that are unlearned and unstable wrest, as they do also the other scriptures, unto their own destruction.

17 Ye therefore, beloved, seeing ye know these things before, beware lest ye also, being led away with the error of the wicked, fall from your own stedfastness.

18 But grow in grace, and in the knowledge of our Lord and Saviour Jesus Christ. To him be glory both now and for ever. Amen.

We listed this whole passage in 2 Peter Chapter 3, because we want you to see how it has been taken out of context by most, and that **the whole chapter is prophetic in nature**. Yes, even Verse 9 and Verse 18. We underlined Verse 8 because it is scorned by most preachers as not having anything to do with prophecy. With your King James Bible open, and your thinking cap on, let us have a little study of this passage shall we?

First, according to 2 Peter 1:1 we see that the book was written to saved people, as is the whole Bible. "*Simon Peter, a servant and an apostle of Jesus Christ, to them that have obtained like precious faith with us through the righteousness of God and our Saviour Jesus Christ:*"

In Chapter 3, verse 1, Peter wants to stir us up by getting us to remember what was spoken by the prophets as well as by the apostles of the Lord Jesus as we see in verse 2. In verse 3, Peter says there shall come scoffers in the last days who walk after their own desires and lust. I wrote "Preachers" next to that in my Bible because your average preacher today does not believe Christ is coming soon, nor does he preach on prophecy, and in fact hopes Christ does not come soon as it would interfere with his church program! "*Where is the promise of his coming? For since the fathers fell asleep all things continue as they were...*" these scoffers say in verse 4! After all the great men of the past believed Christ would come in their lifetime, others have set dates and were wrong, therefore why believe it anymore? In verse 5, Peter says they are willingly ignorant! In other words, men choose to be ignorant of these prophetic truths. It is one thing to be ignorant, it is quite another to be "willingly ignorant." We are afraid some who read this book will choose to stay ignorant. Now notice in verses 5-7 he is speaking about the creative week of Genesis Chapter one! Do you see it? Then in verse 8 he says, "*But, beloved, be not ignorant of this one thing, that one day is with the Lord as a thousand years, and a thousand years as one day.*"

What we want you to see is that right in the very middle of a prophetic chapter, and right at the end of a passage about the creative week of Genesis 1, verse 8 is stuck in there! (Verses 10-13 go on to speak of the end of this world.) Now we want to ask you, what else can verse 8 possibly mean in light of the laws of context and proper Bible interpretation? We believe it is telling us that those seven days of creation are not only literal, but also prophetic of 1000-year periods of time. What else could it possibly mean? Verse 9 shows the heart of God towards the souls of men in that He does not want people to die and go to hell in light of the fact that the end is coming soon. Verses 10-13 show that He is coming as a thief and that there will be a new earth one day and that we are to be "*looking for and hasting unto the coming of the day of God.*" Verse 14 shows that we are to be striving to be found clean and holy when He comes for us. Verse 15 shows that Peter and Paul both preached this same truth. Verse 18 tells us to grow in grace because of what was said from verses 1-17.

There were many who have believed this in history. Let us give you a few quotes from some men of old concerning these truths.

Irenaeus wrote in 150 A.D. in his book "Against Heresies" "For the day of the Lord is as a thousand years; and in six days created things were completed; **it is evident, therefore, that they will come to an end in the sixth thousand years."**

Bishop Latimer wrote in A.D. 1552 "**The world was ordained to endure, as all learned men affirm, 6000 years.** Now of that number, there are passed 5,552 years [as of 1552], so there is no more left but 448 years." (Till the year 2000)

Lactantius in 300 A.D. Wrote this in his book *Divine Institutions:* "Because all the works of God were finished in six days, **it is necessary that the world should remain in this state six ages, that is six thousand years.** Because having finished the works, He rested on the seventh day and blessed it; it is necessary that at the end of the sixth thousandth year all wickedness should be abolished out of the earth and justice should reign for a thousand years."

Not only did men of old believe in a 6000-year earth and then the Millennium, but look at the following Scriptures:

Hosea 6:1-2

Come, and let us return unto the LORD: for he hath torn, and he will heal us; he hath smitten, and he will bind us up. After two days will he revive us: in the third day he will raise us up, and we shall live in his sight.

After two days is prophetic of the two thousand years of the New Testament. The third day is the one thousand year millennial reign of Christ where Israel will once again be the center of things on earth. My skeptical friend, what else could it mean?

Psalm 90:4

For a thousand years in thy sight are but as yesterday when it is past, and as a watch in the night.

Did you know that Moses spoke this Psalm and that he will be one of the two witnesses during the Tribulation?

Psalms 90:12

So teach us to number our days, that we may apply our hearts unto wisdom.

Matthew 17:1-9

And after six days Jesus taketh Peter, James, and John his brother, and bringeth them up into an high mountain apart, And was transfigured before them: and his face did shine as the sun, and his raiment was white as the light. And, behold, there appeared unto them Moses and Elias talking with him. Then answered Peter, and said unto Jesus, Lord, it is good for us to be here: if thou wilt, let us make here three tabernacles; one for thee, and one for Moses, and one for Elias. While he yet spake, behold, a bright cloud overshadowed them: and behold a voice out of the cloud, which said, This is my beloved Son, in whom I am well pleased; hear ye him.

Here we have the story of the transfiguration. Again, all Scripture has three interpretations, the literal, the typical, and the prophetic. This is a literal event that happened, but it also has figurative lessons to apply to our lives as well as prophetic teaching. Verse 1 says "after six days..." hey, there we have Christ appearing after six prophetic days... which are 6000 years according to II Peter 3:8. In the prophetic light of this passage, we see Jesus coming in the clouds and showing His glory to the three disciples, a type of the rapture. If you are still not convinced, look at the verse just before Chapter 17:

Matthew 16:28

Verily I say unto you, There be some standing here, which shall not taste of death, till they see the Son of man coming in his kingdom.

The Bible goes from this verse to Matthew 17:1. What He is saying is that some will not face death, but will be raptured out of here! The "after six days" in verse 1 is prophetic of 6000 years of history. If that still does not convince you, in verse 3 of Matthew 17, Elijah and Moses show up after the 6000 years and after Christ shows us His glory at the rapture. Hey, they are the two witnesses who show up in Jerusalem after the rapture and are responsible for the conversion of the 144,000 Jews at the middle of the

Tribulation. The Bible is an amazing book!

In this chapter, we have tried to show you the prophetic truth of 2 Peter Chapter 3. We have showed you that the whole chapter is prophetic in nature with verse 8 stuck right in the middle. We have given quotes from some men hundreds of years ago who believed in a 6000-year earth, and then the Sabbath rest for 1000 years. We also gave some other passages of Scripture that shed more light on this day as a thousand year truth. My friend, God punished Israel severely for not remembering the Sabbath. Would He hold them to a higher standard than He would Himself? Remember, God set the precedence for the Sabbath way back in Genesis 1. Do you think there is any chance He is going to miss His Sabbath rest after 6000 years of history? Not on your life! God IS going to have His rest after 6000 years! Check out Hebrews Chapter 4! We believe the Old Testament ended at Calvary when the veil was rent in two and that Calvary was 3993 years since Adam and the Seven-year Tribulation is the final 7 years of the Old Testament yet to come.

Now before closing this chapter, let us look at the seven days of the creative week back in Genesis 1 and see how they relate to each of the 1000 year periods of history.

DAY 1: 4000 B.C. — 3000 B.C.

On the first day of creation (check Ussher's date 4004 B.C. in a Scofield Bible) God divided the light from the darkness. It was at the beginning of the first 1000 years of human history that Adam and Eve chose between good and evil and fell from favor with God.

DAY 2: 3000 B.C. — 2000 B.C.

It was on the second creative day that God divided the waters of the firmament. The first firmament (Pre-flood) divided the Earth's atmosphere with what we know as space or outer space. The second firmament still forms the barrier between outer space and the Father's House (the third heaven). Can you think of anything that happened during the second 1000 years of human history that had anything to do with water? How about the Flood of Noah's day where the firmament was broken up and the fountains of the deep were opened up?

DAY 3: 2000 B.C. — 1000 B.C.

On the evening and the morning of the third day, God created the grass and herbs and the fruit trees upon the dry ground. It was at the beginning of the third day of human history (check Ussher's date 2002 B.C. in a Scofield Bible) when God made a covenant with Abraham whereby the nation of Israel was formed. Most preachers agree that the fig tree mentioned throughout the New Testament is a type of Israel.

DAY 4: 1000 B.C. — Christ

On the fourth day of creation, God created the sun, the moon, and the stars, which light the earth. The fourth 1000-year day of human history begins with King David sitting on the throne in Israel and ends with King Jesus the Light of the World. It is also curious to note that most of the Old Testament was written during the last thousand years of the Old Testament Age.

DAY 5: Christ — 1000 A.D.

It was on the fifth creative day that God created the fish

to fill the waters in the seas. Christ commanded His disciples to follow Him and become fishers of men. For years, the symbol of a born-again Christian is none other than the fish.

DAY 6: 1000 A.D. — Present

On the sixth day of creation, God created man; male and female and commanded them to replenish the earth and subdue it. During the last one thousand years while under the curse, mankind has explored, conquered, established, and divided empires. We have explored the earth, the sea, the air, and are currently exploring outer space (God's back yard). Over the last century, we had numerous conflicts, two world wars and are currently working on a third. Today we are but a mere push of a button away from complete annihilation. The book of Daniel has been unsealed. Men are running to and fro and knowledge has been increased. The earth's 1000 year Sabbath is right around the corner, and rest assured, God will remember His Sabbath and keep it holy.

DAY 7: -- The Millennial Reign of King Jesus

Genesis 2:1-2

Thus the heavens and the earth were finished, and all the host of them. And on the seventh day God ended his work which he had made; and he rested on the seventh day from all his work which he had made.

After six 1000-year days, this old sin-cursed earth will finally come to rest with King Jesus sitting on the throne of David ruling and reigning with a rod of iron and the lion shall lie down by the lamb. Praise God!

Seven Clocks a Tickin'

Chapter Six

But of the times and the seasons, brethren, ye have no need that I write unto you For yourselves know perfectly that the day of the Lord so cometh as a thief in the night. For when they shall say, Peace and safety; then sudden destruction cometh upon them, as travail upon a woman with child; and they shall not escape But ye, brethren, are not in darkness, that that day should overtake you as a thief. Ye are all the children of light, and the children of the day: we are not of the night, nor of darkness Therefore let us not sleep, as do others; but let us watch and be sober. For they that sleep sleep in the night; and they that be drunken are drunken in the night. But let us, who are of the day, be sober, putting on the breastplate of faith and love; and for an helmet, the hope of salvation. For God hath not appointed us to wrath, but to obtain salvation by our Lord Jesus Christ, Who died for us, that, whether we wake or sleep, we should live together with him. 1 Thessalonians 5:1-10

There are at least seven clocks ticking that are all pointing towards a major event coming in our day. We do not know the date of the rapture; we believe it is imminent. Christ could come at any moment. However, there are seven clocks ticking away and they all point towards a climatic event coming in our generation.

In light of the fact that the Bible teaches there will be

6000 years of human history, and then a 1000-year Sabbath rest, we must be very close to the rapture. We believe we are near the year 2000 of the New Testament Age on God's calendar. God does not use the solar calendar; He uses the 360-day prophetic calendar. It is right now somewhere close to the year 2000 on God's calendar if you start with Calvary to the present with 360-day years. The New Testament did not start at the birth of Christ, it started at Calvary as discussed in another chapter.

We want to share with you seven clocks that are ticking towards a major event in our generation. These events certainly line up with Scripture as far as the Tribulation is concerned, but you will have to use your own judgment as to what these clocks may mean. As our text above tells us, we are not to be taken as a thief but are to see the day approaching and be prepared for the rapture. It is like a couple when they find out they are going to have a baby. They are very excited, they begin telling others that they are expecting, they begin preparing their home for the new arrival, but they do not pack the suitcase until after the 8th or 9th month when the "signs" begin to appear. My friend, we believe the signs all point to the fact that we are near the end of the age and we had better have our bags packed and the gas tank full!

There are seven clocks a tickin' that all point towards a soon climactic event:

I. Daniel's Clock a Tickin'

Daniel's clock is ticking away. Daniel talked about the

revived Roman Empire that will be ruled by the Antichrist and we are on the verge of that right now. The term "global" is a household word even now. We hear about global markets, global currency, global trade, and global unity. The whole world is tied together through the internet, stock market, and trade. Daniel's 70th week is just a trumpet sound away. The whole world is now ready for globalism. Look at the following quotes concerning "globalism."

"Globalization is the central reality of our time. It is coming and you can't stop it!"

Bill Clinton State of the Union Address, January, 2000

"If one word encapsulates the changes we are living through, it is globalization. It is the future of the world as we know it."

Former secretary general of the United Nation, Kofi Annan

Back in the year 2000, the prime ministers of great Britain, the Netherlands, Sweden, and the chancellor of Germany all banded together to collectively write, "We all embrace the potential of globalization. It is the future of the world as we know it."

"The New Left Takes on the World" Washington Post, September 6, 2000, p. A19

II. Blood Red Moon Clock a Tickin'

And I will shew wonders in heaven above, and signs in the earth beneath; blood, and fire, and vapour of smoke: The sun shall be turned into darkness, and the moon into blood, before that great and notable day of the Lord come: (Acts 2:19-20)

And there shall be signs in the sun, and in the moon, and in the stars; and upon the earth distress of nations, with perplexity; the sea and the waves roaring; (Luke 21:25)

There are four blood red moons that appear in 2014 and 2015 that many are talking about today. Let me explain these lunar eclipses or, blood red moons as they are called.

1. A blood red moon is a total lunar eclipse.

A partial lunar eclipse is never called a blood red moon. Only a total lunar eclipse is considered a blood red moon. It is caused when the earth gets between the sun and the moon. The moon appears "red" because of the rays of the sun going through the earth's atmosphere.

2. A "tetrad" is four consecutive TOTAL lunar eclipses in a row.

There have been many blood red moons (total lunar eclipses) throughout history. There is nothing at all unusual about a lunar eclipse occurring. There have also been several tetrads throughout history. Though not real common, it is nothing all that unusual either. Let me be sure you understand, a tetrad is four TOTAL lunar eclipses in a row. Three total lunar eclipses and one partial lunar eclipse would not be considered a tetrad in the scientific community.

3. An extremely rare tetrad is taking place in 2014/2015.

Remember, a "tetrad" is a scientific term that simply means four total lunar eclipses in a row. What is rare in

2014/2015 is the fact that these four lunar eclipses occur on Feast of Passover and Feast of Tabernacles in 2014/2015. Two years in a row, a full lunar eclipse on these two same feast days. Now, this has my attention! Is it getting your attention?

4. **There are some interesting and prophetic lessons about the occurrence of blood moons on Jewish Feast days.**

Passover is the first and Tabernacles is the last of the Seven Feasts of the Lord discussed in chapter seven of this book. It is also interesting that the seven feasts all take place in a space of seven months. (Nisan - Tishri) If I don't have you on the edge of your seat now, you are just not thinking! Seven is God's number of completion. There are seven churches in Revelation, seven trumpets, seven angels, seven seals, seven vials, seven days of creation. I believe there will be seven thousand years of human history. The Tribulation is seven years. There are seven days in a week. Now we learn that there is a blood red moon on the 1st and 7th of the seven feasts that take place in the first seven months of the Jewish calendar? Yes, this has got my attention! But wait, there is more…much more.

5. **There have been seven tetrads in the whole 2000 year New Testament Age where the blood red moons fell on the Jewish feasts of Passover and Tabernacles.**

Seven times in the last 2000 years there has been a rare occurrence of these four back-to-back full lunar blood red moons on the feasts of Passover and Tabernacles. Have I still got your attention? I have checked this out on the

NASA website myself.

6. There is an eighth tetrad in 2014/2015.

Make sure you understand what I am telling you. Seven times in the entire New Testament Age there has been a tetrad on these same two feast days. Each occurrence was on Passover and Tabernacles two consecutive years in a row. In the last 2000 years this has only happened seven times. There is an eighth occurrence coming in 2014/2015.

7. Each of the first seven tetrads are associated with an important historical event that corresponded to Israel.

Since the seven tetrads all revolved around Israel, it is very possible that the eighth will too. In fact, I would say it is more than possible, I would say it is almost a certainty. Let's look at the tetrads throughout history that fell on Jewish feast days and see what we can learn. There will no doubt be some prophetic lessons for us.

Here are the dates of all eight tetrads that occur from Calvary to the end of the 21st century:

A. 162/163 A.D.

B. 795/796 A.D.

C. 842/843 A.D.

D. 860/861 A.D.

There were some historical events for Israel during these first four tetrad years but we will not take the time to discuss them. They are certainly not as significant as the ones to follow so I will not take the time on them.

However, I assure you there is a connection to Israel in these first four. The following are quite significant and I want us to look at them.

E. 1493/1494 A.D.

In 1492 Columbus left Spain to discover the new world. He is credited with finding America which God raised up for two purposes. First, America would be used to spread the gospel around the world. Second, God would use America to protect and be a future haven for the Jews. In 1493 King Ferdinand and Queen Isabella of Spain ordered all Jewish people to leave the country. They were given 14 days to get out and could only take what they could carry. (The Spanish Inquisition also was begun a few years prior and continued on for many years.) A few months after the Jews were expelled from Spain, the series of blood red moons began in Israel. All total lunar eclipses and all on Passover and Tabernacles for two consecutive years.

F. 1949/1950 A.D.

Israel returned to the land of Israel in May of 1948. However, they fought a war for several months with the surrounding Arab nations before they officially seated their new government. They also got a seat on the United Nations in January of 1949. Passover was four months later and began the series of four blood red moons. Again, all four were full lunar eclipses and all on the Feast of Passover and Tabernacles for two consecutive years.

G. 1967/1968 A.D.

In June of 1967, Israel was attacked once again. It was

a miraculous victory for the Jews that resulted in the acquiring of Gaza and the Golan Heights as well as Jerusalem. It is called the Six-Day War. On Passover in April of 1967 began the first of four blood red moons. All four were full lunar eclipses and all four fell on the same two feasts of Passover and Tabernacles. This tetrad began two months before the Six-Day War.

H. 2014/2015 A.D.

This eighth tetrad is occurring now and on those same feast days. There will be a blood red moon on Feast of Passover April 15th in 2014. Then on Tabernacles the same year. The same on Passover and Tabernacles in 2015. There are no more of these "tetrads" on Jewish feast days for the rest of this century. By the way, there are also two solar eclipses coming in Israel with the first on March 20th, 2015. That is the 1st of Nisan which is 14 days before Passover. The second solar eclipse is seven months later on September 13th which is Feast of Trumpets. Is it interesting that the two solar eclipses are on the same first and last of the seven months? In 2014/2015 we not only have the four blood red moons on Jewish feast days, but we have two solar eclipses and one of them is on a feast day!

So what does all this mean? In the Bible the moon seems to be a sign for the nation of Israel. **There have only been seven Blood Moon Tetrads on these feast days between Jesus Christ's first coming and 2013**. Remember, we are talking about total lunar eclipses on the feasts of Passover and Tabernacles two consecutive years in a row making them a very rare event that scientists call a tetrad. Each and every time there was some significant event which impacted the Jewish people. All seven times that it has happened in the last 2000 years something happened concerning the Jews. Seven times this rare occurrence fell on the first and last of the seven feasts that are in a seven month period on the Jewish calendar and we have preachers around the country scoffing at it? Can you believe that?

Seven is God's number of completion. The 8th occurrence of a tetrad began on Passover, April 15th 2014. Then a blood red moon on Feast of Tabernacles October the 8th and the same occurrence on the same two feasts in 2015. Eight is the number of man. It is also the number of new beginnings. When the whole earth was covered with the flood, Noah "the eighth person" (2 Peter 2:5) stepped out of the ark to commence a new order of things. "Eight souls" (1 Peter 3:20) were saved from the flood and replenished the earth. It was a new beginning.

I am not saying the rapture is coming as a result of these blood red moons, I am saying it most likely has something to do with Israel. Something may take place concerning Israel during or shortly after the blood red moons. Since three of these blood moons have passed at the writing of this chapter, it is becoming more obvious that something big is in fact happening. Israel is surrounded by enemies and even America has turned its back on her. Now, the rapture would certainly be a big event for Israel because it sets up the rise of Antichrist and the seven-year covenant with them. Again, I am not saying that is what is coming. I am saying that something always happened concerning Israel at the time of these four blood red moons in history. I believe there could be something big this time as well.

Here are the dates of the blood red moons and solar eclipses from NASA website as they occur in 2014-2015.

* Passover - April 15, 2014
* Tabernacles - October 8, 2014
* Passover - April 4, 2015
* Tabernacles - September. 28, 2015

Two solar eclipses:

* March 20, 2015 (14 days before Passover, 1st of Nisan)
* September 13, 2015 (Eve of Feast of Trumpets 29th of Elul)

III. Jubilee Clock a Tickin'

There have been 69 jubilee cycles since instituted in Leviticus Chapter 25 in 1500 BC. If you add 1500 years of the Old Testament and 2000 years of the New Testament you get 3500 years. A Jubilee happens every 49 years with the entire 50th year as a Sabbath. If you divide 3500 by 50 you get 70 Jubilees. The next Jubilee will be the 70th. I believe it will be the final Jubilee and that Christ will return on the white horse in Revelation 19:11 and take back the earth. We are tickin' towards that final 70th Jubilee. (See chapter eight for more on this subject.)

IV. Church Age Clock a Tickin'

If you study the Seven Churches mentioned in Revelation chapter two and three, you will find that they are not only literal churches that existed in John's day, but are also prophetic of the entire Church Age.

CHART OF THE SEVEN AGES OF CHURCH HISTORY

Ephesus	**Means desirable one – 1st**
Smyrna	**Comes from the word myrrh, signifying suffering ... 100-300**
Pergamos	**Means marriage, as in married to the state or world . . . 300-500**
Thyatira	**Means continual sacrifice, (works, mass, ceremonies, dark ages, etc.) 500-1500**
Sardis	**Means remnant . . . and we see this during the reformation period . . . 1500-1700**
Philadelphia	**Brotherly love . . . Great awakenings, revivals, Edwards, Whitefield . . . 1700-1901**
Laodicean	**The rights of the people . . just look around today! 1901 - Rapture**

*** Dates are approximate**

Brief Summary of the Seven Ages of the Church

The church in Ephesus represents the first 100 years of history, also called the Apostolic Age. This is during the days of the Apostles, including Paul's missionary journeys.

The church in Smyrna represents the next 200 years from 100-313 when Constantine showed up. It is said that Polycarp, a convert of John, was the pastor in Smyrna. History gives us record of ten Roman Emperors who persecuted the church during this time. Compare that to Revelation 2:10 *Fear none of those things which thou shalt suffer: behold, the devil shall cast some of you into prison, that ye may be tried; and ye shall have tribulation ten days....* Nero was the first of those ten wicked emperors who brought terrible persecution to the church. In A.D. 156 Polycarp was given the choice to revile Christ or be burned at the stake to which he made this famous reply: "*Eighty and six years have I served him and He never did me any harm; how then can I blaspheme my King and my Saviour?*"

The church in Pergamos represents the age from 313 to 590. Pergamos is defined "marriage." The Church united with the state or the world if you will. The church became the state religion, and the political leader, Constantine, became the religious leader. Much of Catholic doctrine stems from this age, including the practice of the doctrines of Balaam and the Nicolaitans.

The church in Thyatira represents the age from 590-

1500's also known as "The Dark Ages." The name Thyatira means "continual sacrifice." It symbolizes the works, ceremonies, and rituals such as "the mass" and Mary worship and good deeds that were added to the gospel. The church in Sardis represents the Reformation Age from 1500-1700 during the times of Luther, Calvin, and others. The printing press was invented in 1550 with a Bible being the first complete book ever printed! The Bible in the hands of the common man soon opened many of the people's eyes to the truth. Be very careful about following someone who thinks that the Bible is a book for the "clergy" and not the common man. 2 Peter 1:20-21 *Knowing this first, that no prophecy of the scripture is of any private interpretation. For the prophecy came not in old time by the will of man: but holy men of God spake as they were moved by the Holy Ghost.*

The church in Philadelphia covers 1700's-1901 and is the time of great revivals and the two great awakenings. Philadelphia means "brotherly love." God raised up some great men like George Whitefield, and Jonathan Edwards, who preached the famous sermon "Sinners in the Hand's of an Angry God." Men like Spurgeon and Moody shook whole continents for God in the 1800's! America arose as the Christian nation of the world. To this day, she still sends out more fundamental Christian missionaries than any other nation.

The church in Laodicea covers 1901 until the rapture. This age is by far the worst of them all. Why 1901 you might ask? It is the very year that the RSV translation of the Bible came to America. For the first time in our great American history, we now had two authorities, two Bibles.

It has been downhill from there ever since. Just look at Revelation 3:14-20 and see if it is not describing our churches today. There has not been much revival to speak of since 1901. Our churches are cold, our people are pleasure seekers, proud, unfaithful, covetous, and of very little conviction. We have become tarnished by sin and immorality. People are easily offended, and preachers are either running off with the secretary or refusing to preach against sin. The Ecumenical Movement has infiltrated the church with false doctrine which will one day lead to a worship of the Antichrist! We had better get ready, the trumpet is about to sound, and the rapture could occur at any moment. All things are now ready. How about you, are you ready to meet the Lord?

V. Nuclear Clock a Tickin'

For the first time ever, in our generation, the world has the capability to destroy itself. Never before has that been possible. When George Washington read the following passage in 1776, do you suppose it made much sense to him as he looked at his old flintlock?

For then shall be great tribulation, such as was not since the beginning of the world to this time, no, nor ever shall be. And except those days should be shortened, there should no flesh be saved: but for the elect's sake those days shall be shortened. Matthew 24:21-22

We can understand this very well today though. It is believed that Russia has at least 10,000 ICBM's aimed at America right now. Each one of them is more powerful than the bombs dropped on Japan in 1945. Can you comprehend that? We have read that America has weapons that we have not even tested because we are not sure how powerful and destructive they are! More and more countries are getting nukes. It is believed North Korea has them; Iran will shortly have them. It is just a matter of time before tragedy strikes. It is possible that Israel could be annihilated in a moment. Now we know from the Bible that will not happen, which leads us to believe the rapture is soon, as Israel has more enemies today than ever before. Even America has lost favor with God as we bargain away the land of Israel and foolishly attempt to make a Palestinian State.

VI. 7000 Year Clock a Tickin'

If the world is going to last 6000 years, and then God has a Sabbath rest, then we are at the door! We believe there have been 3993 years from Adam to Calvary. 7 years of Old Testament are yet to come during the Tribulation, or Daniel's 70th week. You see all 70 of those weeks of years mentioned in the Old Testament.

Daniel 9:24

Seventy weeks are determined upon thy people and upon thy holy city, to finish the transgression, and to make an end of sins, and to make reconciliation for iniquity, and to bring in everlasting righteousness, and to seal up the vision and prophecy, and to anoint the most Holy.

When Messiah was "cut off" at Calvary, Israel's clock stopped, and the New Testament Age clock began. If we use the 360-year clock that God uses, we are now very close to the end of that 2000-year clock that started at Calvary.

√ The Seven-year Tribulation will complete the 4000-year-Old Testament clock, and we are near the end of the New Testament clock, leaving the 1000 year Millennium to complete the 7000 years of human history. We are almost at the door my friend; you had better have your bags packed and the gas tank full! In fact, maybe we had better leave the car running!

VII. Israel's Clock A Tickin'

√ Matthew 24:32-34

Now learn a parable of the fig tree; When his branch is yet tender, and putteth forth leaves, ye know that summer is nigh: So likewise ye, when ye shall see all these things, know that it is near, even at the doors. Verily I say unto you, This generation shall not pass, till all these things be fulfilled.

Most people believe the Fig tree represents Israel. This passage is a prophecy about the restoration of the nation of Israel, which took place in 1948. However, they got Jerusalem in the six-day war of 1967. A generation is somewhere around 50 years, which happens to be a Jubilee. Brethren, we are near the end of this clock as well.

These are seven clocks a tickin'. We are sure there are others.

How is your "clock?" Are you redeeming the time that God has given you? Are you busy for the Lord? This is no time to be backslidden! If you are ever going to do something for God, you better get doing it!

The Seven Feasts

Chapter Seven

In the Bible we learn that Israel had seven major feasts. As you will see, it is amazing how these feasts are symbolic of future events. The first four feasts symbolize events that have already taken place. The last three are symbolic of events yet to come, and take place four months after the Feast of Pentecost. (The 4th feast) Christ fulfilled the first four right to the exact day. Will the last three be fulfilled on their exact day? It is certainly possibly, and in fact probable since we know He is a God of order.

Here is a list of the seven feasts and when they occurred. To measure time, Israel did not use the sun, as we do today. They used the 354-day lunar-based calendar adding a month every few years. Each month started with the new moon and was approximately 30 days long. Nisan was changed to the 1st month of their year as recorded in Exodus 12. Nisan is usually in our month of April, but sometimes in March. As you can see in the chart, there is a four-month gap where the people did not come together for any feasts. The reason for this is they were working in the fields preparing a harvest. The Feast of Trumpets is all about blowing the trumpet for assembling and gathering the harvest. That is interesting in light of the rapture being a harvest of souls is it not.

Feast of Passover	Nisan 10th-14th (Our March or April)
Feast of Unleavened bread	Nisan 15th-21st, 7 days after Passover
Feast of Firstfruits	First day of week after Passover
Feast of Pentecost	50 days after Passover FOUR MONTH GAP HERE
Feast of Trumpets	1st day of seventh month
Feast of Day of Atonement	10th day of seventh month
Feast of Tabernacles	15th day of seventh month

Now let us look at these seven feasts and see how they apply to us in the light of prophecy. On the Feast of Passover, exactly at the right time, Christ our Passover Lamb (I Cor 5:7) went to the cross and paid in full the sin debt of the world. This took place 483 years (69 weeks), after the command to build the wall in Nehemiah as explained in the book of Daniel. You see, nobody knew the date of the birth of Christ, but anyone who studied Daniel knew exactly when Messiah would be cut off. The birth of Christ was a mystery revealed only to Joseph and Mary and a few shepherds. We do not believe even Satan knew who Christ was until John baptized Him. The wise men did not show up until 2 years later.

You see, Christmas came from the Catholic Church and

has thrown us off for centuries. It is not the birth of Christ that is important, but rather the death of Christ. The New Testament did not start at the birth of Christ, but at the death of Christ. The truth is Satan was probably watching John the Baptist, thinking he was the Messiah. Do you have any other explanation for the fact that John was filled with the Holy Ghost from his mother's womb? That has baffled preachers for years! We believe it was for the purpose of throwing off the Devil! John was a decoy.

On what we call "Palm Sunday" Christ rode into Jerusalem on a donkey and presented Himself to the people as a perfect sacrificial lamb. He fulfilled all the requirements of Exodus 12. The people watched Him for four days just as they were instructed in Exodus 12. After the four days, the Lamb of God was put on a cross; He shed His blood and died. He was put in the tomb by 6:00 P.M., which is the beginning of the next day, which would be Thursday.

This was the beginning of the next feast, Unleavened Bread. Christ was in the tomb to prove He was pure and sinless and that His body did not see corruption during this feast. Christ rose on the exact day of the Feast of Firstfruits which began on Nisan 17th, Sunday. This happened at 6:00 P.M. Saturday night, which is Sunday on their clock. Christ was in the tomb from 6:00 P.M. Wed to 6:00 P.M. Saturday night which is Sunday.

The next feast is Pentecost, which is 50 days after Feast of Firstfruits. We see what happened here in Acts Chapter 2. Christ empowered His church to go out and plant a harvest. That is what this feast was all about. It was to encourage and prepare the people to get out in the fields and get a crop in the ground. Christ empowered His church to go out and plant the seed of the Word of God to get a harvest of souls, to get a BRIDE for Jesus Christ! Do you see how each of these first four feasts were fulfilled right to the exact day and that they all picture something that has already happened?

Now hang on to your seat! There are three more feasts, and these picture future events. Let us ask you, what is the next event on God's calendar? That is right, the rapture. What does the Bible say about the rapture? Something about trumpets right? I Thessalonians 4:15-18, Revelation 4:1 and I Corinthians 15:52 all speak of the rapture occurring with the sound of a trumpet. We believe the Feast of Trumpets is symbolic of the rapture.

(1 Thessalonians 4:15-18) *For this we say unto you by the word of the Lord, that we which are alive and remain unto the coming of the Lord shall not prevent them which are asleep. For the Lord himself shall descend from heaven with a shout, with the voice of the archangel, and with the trump of God: and the dead in Christ shall rise first: Then we which are alive and remain shall be caught up together with them in the clouds, to meet the Lord in the air: and so shall we ever be with the Lord. Wherefore comfort one another with these words.*

Revelation 4:1 *After this I looked, and, behold, a door was opened in heaven: and the first voice which I heard was as it were of a trumpet talking with me; which said, Come up hither, and I will shew thee things which must be hereafter.*

1 Corinthians 15:52 *In a moment, in the twinkling of an eye, at the last trump: for the trumpet shall sound, and the dead shall be raised incorruptible, and we shall be changed.*

In Bible days, the trumpet was blown to assemble the people. They would blow trumpets on the Feast of Trumpets to assemble the people at the harvest time. Now the first four feasts all happened on the exact day of the feasts. Does that mean the rapture will happen on Feast of Trumpets? We do not know, but it could. It sure makes logical sense doesn't it? However, we believe we are to be looking for Him every day. By the way, here is an interesting bit of information about the Feast of Trumpets. It occurs at the new moon, which is the first day of the seventh month of Tishri. (It would be in our months of Sept. or Oct.) Did you know that it is believed by many, including Bishop Ussher who wrote the dates that are in the Scofield Bible, that the world was created in Genesis 1 on Tishri 1? Tishri 1, the Feast of Trumpets, is also the Jewish New Year! Wow, in light of that, it makes sense why God would instruct the Jews to make that their new year's day.

Now this also backs up the 6000-year earth and then the Sabbath rest belief. If creation started on Tishri 1, and IF Christ were to come on Trumpets, it would be EXACTLY 6000 YEARS of human history! We do not mean around or nearly, we mean exactly 6000 years. (Once you add in the Seven-year Tribulation) After Trumpets, ten days later, is the Day of Atonement, also called Yom Kippur. It is a most holy day for the Jews. It was the one time of the year that the High Priest could enter the Holy of Holies and offer the sacrifice. We believe it looks forward to the Second coming of Christ when He comes at the end of the Tribulation and stands on the Mountain of Olives as was prophesied in Acts 1:11-12 where Christ comes back as King of Kings and Lord of Lords! *Which also said, Ye men of Galilee, why stand ye gazing up into heaven? this same Jesus, which is taken up from you into heaven, shall so come in like manner as ye have seen him go into heaven. Then returned they unto Jerusalem from the mount called Olivet, which is from Jerusalem a Sabbath day's journey.*

Jesus became our High Priest when the veil was rent.

Hebrews 3:1 Wherefore, holy brethren, partakers of the heavenly calling, consider the Apostle and High Priest of our profession, Christ Jesus;

Hebrews 4:14 Seeing then that we have a great high priest, that is passed into the heavens, Jesus the Son of God, let us hold fast our profession.

15 For we have not an high priest which cannot be touched with the feeling of our infirmities; but was in all points tempted like as we are, yet without sin.

16 Let us therefore come boldly unto the throne of grace, that we may obtain mercy, and find grace to help in time of need

Hebrews 6:20 Whither the forerunner is for us entered, even Jesus, made an high priest for ever after the order of Melchisedec.

Lev 23

The last feast is called Tabernacles where the people would gather and dwell in tents, also called booths. It is five days after Atonement. It was a time of rest after the harvest, and is a type of the 1000-year Sabbath rest called the Millennium. These last three feasts all take place in their 7th month, which is our September or October. It is harvest time; it was in the Fall.

We trust that these truths will be an encouragement to you. The Lord is coming back. We are to be watching for Him. May we be found faithful when He comes for us!

OCT 5 is 8th day

"Doubtless much which is designedly obscure to us will be clear to those for whom it was written as the time approaches."

~C.I. Scofield

God's Final Jubilee

Chapter Eight

"And thou shalt number seven sabbaths of years unto thee, seven times seven years; and the space of the seven sabbaths of years shall be unto thee forty and nine years. Then shalt thou cause the trumpet of the jubile to sound on the tenth day of the seventh month, in the day of atonement shall ye make the trumpet sound throughout all your land. And ye shall hallow the fiftieth year, and proclaim liberty throughout all the land unto all the inhabitants thereof: it shall be a jubile unto you; and ye shall return every man unto his possession, and ye shall return every man unto his family. A jubile shall that fiftieth year be unto you: ye shall not sow, neither reap that which groweth of itself in it, nor gather the grapes in it of thy vine undressed. For it is the jubile; it shall be holy unto you: ye shall eat the increase thereof out of the field. In the year of this jubile ye shall return every man unto his possession." (Leviticus 25:8-13)

Apart from the seven feasts, nothing will do more for your understanding of prophecy than the information about the Jubilee in this chapter. **The seven feasts are so important to understanding it all. They are the key that unlocks the door to prophecy. They are God's prophetic calendar and the jubilee plays an important part in these feasts.**

There is a Jubilee coming. The Jubilee is a Sabbath. There are several Sabbaths in the Bible, but three major ones I want you to understand.

1. The seventh day of the week is a Sabbath.

"Remember the sabbath day, to keep it holy. Six days shalt thou labour, and do all thy work: But the seventh day is the sabbath of the LORD thy God: in it thou shalt not do any work, thou, nor thy son, nor thy daughter, thy manservant, nor thy maidservant, nor thy cattle, nor thy stranger that is within thy gates: For in six days the LORD made heaven and earth, the sea, and all that in them is, and rested the seventh day: wherefore the LORD blessed the sabbath day, and hallowed it." (Exodus 20:8-11)

This is a Sabbath for man. It is a day for man to rest from all his labors. It is also figurative. For instance, in the book of Numbers a man was put to death for picking up sticks on the Sabbath. The Sabbath is a picture of resting in Christ for our salvation. Picking up sticks was a type of working and not trusting fully in Messiah for salvation. If you truly want to place yourself under the Old Testament Sabbath and keep the Sabbath in a scriptural manner, you cannot even pick up sticks for your fire, or cook or do any labor. You cannot even travel. There certainly is a principle taught here that man needs to rest from his labor once each week, but man is no longer under the Sabbath of the law.

2. The seventh year is a Sabbath for the land.

"Speak unto the children of Israel, and say unto them, When ye come into the land which I give you, then shall the land

keep a sabbath unto the LORD. Six years thou shalt sow thy field, and six years thou shalt prune thy vineyard, and gather in the fruit thereof; But in the seventh year shall be a sabbath of rest unto the land, a sabbath for the LORD: thou shalt neither sow thy field, nor prune thy vineyard." (Leviticus 25:2-4)

This was God's plan for restoring the land. Over time, the nutrients will become depleted from the soil. God ordained that in the sixth year they would harvest twice the crop. In the seventh year they would let the land rest. They would live off the double harvest from the year before. The people had to trust in the Lord to operate under His system. It also was a time that the servants as well as the animals would rest. This is the Sabbath that Israel had broken that brought about the seventy-year captivity that we read about in 2 Chronicles 36:20-21 as well as the book of Daniel.

3. The 49th year is a Sabbath called the Jubilee.

"And thou shalt number seven sabbaths of years unto thee, seven times seven years; and the space of the seven sabbaths of years shall be unto thee forty and nine years. Then shalt thou cause the trumpet of the jubile to sound on the tenth day of the seventh month, in the day of atonement shall ye make the trumpet sound throughout all your land." (Leviticus 25:8-9)

Every seventh day is a Sabbath for man to rest. Every seventh year was a Sabbath for the land to rest. After the 49th year (7x7 years) it was a Jubilee. Not only was it a rest for the land, but it was a proclamation of liberty throughout

10th day
Sept 23-15 yom Kipper

the land. In that day a trumpet was sounded and the whole 50th year was proclaimed as a Jubilee. Several things happened at the Jubilee. These are very prophetic of things to come so don't miss it.

a. All property went back to the original owner on the Jubilee.

Leviticus 25:13, this is how the Lord kept the land in the possession of the original twelve tribes as appointed under Joshua. According to Leviticus Chapter 25, the Jubilee is begun at the end of the 49th year on the Day of Atonement which is the sixth feast! *"Then shalt thou cause the trumpet of the jubile to sound on the tenth day of the seventh month, in the day of atonement shall ye make the trumpet sound throughout all your land." (Leviticus 25:9)*

Every 49 years on the Day of Atonement, the trumpet is sounded and the entire 50th year is a Jubilee year. Has it hit you yet? Prophetically, the Day of Atonement is the day that Christ comes back to the earth on the white horse at the end of the Tribulation and puts down the Antichrist and liberates the earth.

"And I saw heaven opened, and behold a white horse; and he that sat upon him was called Faithful and True, and in righteousness he doth judge and make war. His eyes were as a flame of fire, and on his head were many crowns; and he had a name written, that no man knew, but he himself. And he was clothed with a vesture dipped in blood: and his name is called The Word of God. And the armies which were in heaven followed him upon white horses, clothed in fine linen, white and clean. And out of his mouth goeth a

sharp sword, that with it he should smite the nations: and he shall rule them with a rod of iron: and he treadeth the winepress of the fierceness and wrath of Almighty God. And he hath on his vesture and on his thigh a name written, KING OF KINGS, AND LORD OF LORDS." (Revelation 19:11-16)

Since Christ is the original owner of the earth, can you see the significance of the Jubilee in regards to the second coming? "*The land shall not be sold for ever: for the land is mine; for ye are strangers and sojourners with me." (Leviticus 25:23)*

I believe Christ will fulfill not only the Day of Atonement, but the Jubilee as well and will do so on the very same day! All property goes back to the original owner every 50 years. If you sold your property the year before, it now belongs to you again. Obviously, anyone buying property understood this and would not have paid much for it. Basically they were leasing the property. This is God's plan.

b. All debt was forgiven on the Jubilee.

Wow, how do you like that? If you were in debt, it was forgiven on the day of Jubilee. This gave all men a fresh start at life. It also kept the lenders in check. For instance, if the Jubilee is just a few months or years away, would you be giving a ten year loan to someone? So, the Jubilee even had a way of keeping debt under control.

c. All bond slaves were set free on the Jubilee.

If you had gone into debt and sold yourself as a bond slave to pay your debt, you and your family would go free at the Jubilee.

Now, these things are a prophetic picture of what Jesus has done for the sinner, and what He is coming to do at His second coming. When we trust Christ for salvation, He sets us free from the penalty and payment of sin that we owe. He wipes the slate clean! Liberty is achieved. We were bond servants and slaves to sin but now we are set free. The Jubilee is a type of this, but there is more. You see, since the earth was also cursed when man sinned, it too must be redeemed. This will happen during the Tribulation. **At the final day when Christ comes back to the earth on the Day of Atonement, I believe it will be a Jubilee year and Christ will have the seven-sealed book in His hand and will stand on the Mountain of Olives and will proclaim liberty and will take back possession of the earth**. *"The earth is the LORD'S, and the fulness thereof; the world, and they that dwell therein."* (Psalms 24:1)

Some observations to consider:

1. The Jubilee is very prophetic.

Everything God set up has a purpose and a meaning. The Jubilee fits the second coming of Christ perfectly! At the Jubilee all debt is forgiven, all bond servants are made free, and all property goes back to the original owner. This is all fulfilled completely at the return of the Lord.

2. We are approaching the 70th Jubilee.

There is that number seven again. Moses was given the instructions about the Jubilee approximately 1500 B.C. We will have 2000 years in the New Testament Age. That makes 3500 years total. Each Jubilee cycle is 50 years total. If you divide 3500 by 50, you get 70 Jubilees. I realize Israel has not kept the Jubilee in hundreds of years, but I have no doubt that the Lord has kept up with it. After all, it is a Sabbath, right? God kept up with the Sabbaths that the children of Israel profaned and gave them seventy years of captivity in Babylon as a result of it. The next Jubilee on the near horizon is the 70th Jubilee.

3. We are approaching on the 120th Jubilee from Adam.

From the time of Adam until now is 120 Jubilee periods of 50 years each. I realize that the Jubilee did not officially start until 1500 B.C. However, did you know that if you go back and start at Genesis 1 and count until the end of the 2000th year of the New Testament you get 6000 years? If you divide 6000 by 50 you get 120 Jubilee cycles. Is that interesting? Consider this passage of Scripture in light of that.

And it came to pass, when men began to multiply on the face of the earth, and daughters were born unto them, That the sons of God saw the daughters of men that they were fair; and they took them wives of all which they chose. And the LORD said, My spirit shall not always strive with man, for that he also is flesh: yet his days shall be an hundred and twenty years. There were giants in the earth in those days; and also after that, when the sons of God came in unto the daughters of men, and they bare children to them, the same became mighty men which were of old, men of renown. (Genesis 6:1-4)

We are not going to get into the discussion of who the sons of God were. What I do want you to look at is the verse I underlined. Notice that God says man's days shall be 120 years. Most folks think that is talking about the years Noah spent building the ark. That is what I believed for many years. Problem with that is, it is not accurate. Noah spent no more than 100 years building the ark. We see here that Noah was 500 years of age when his children began to be born. "*And Noah was five hundred years old: and Noah begat Shem, Ham, and Japheth.*" (Genesis 5:32)

"*These are the generations of Noah: Noah was a just man and perfect in his generations, and Noah walked with God. And Noah begat three sons, Shem, Ham, and Japheth. The earth also was corrupt before God, and the earth was filled with violence. And God looked upon the earth, and, behold, it was corrupt; for all flesh had corrupted his way upon the earth. And God said unto Noah, The end of all flesh is come before me; for the earth is filled with violence through them; and, behold, I will destroy them with the earth. Make thee an ark of gopher wood; rooms shalt thou make in the ark, and shalt pitch it within and without with pitch.*" (Genesis 6:9-14)

The command to build the ark was obviously given AFTER Noah's three sons were born. (Genesis 7:6) "*And Noah was six hundred years old when the flood of waters was upon the earth.*" It is plain that Noah was commanded to build the ark AFTER he was 500 years old and AFTER his three sons were born. Then we see that the rains began when Noah was 600 years old. That means Noah was 100 years or less building the ark.

Now, I want to give you a theory about what I believe God is telling us in the passage. It is my opinion that God is telling us that His Spirit is going to dwell with man upon the earth for 120 generations and I believe a generation is 50 years. 120 generations of 50-year periods would be 6000 years. If I am right about this, then God was saying that there will be 120 Jubilees making up 6000 years and then the end. My friend, the next Jubilee on the time clock of Heaven will be the 120th from Adam.

When is God's Final Jubilee

Obviously, the big question on the minds of everyone reading this chapter is, "When is this final Jubilee scheduled to happen?" I have to be honest and tell you that nobody knows for sure. I am not a date setter. The calendar is so messed up I do not think we can be sure of anything. The Israelites have not kept a Jubilee in over 2000 years. I have done some study on it and nobody is sure what year Israel kept its last Jubilee. The purpose of this book is not to set a date, but rather to get you to see we are close. However, let me share some possibilities with you about when the final Jubilee may occur.

There are many prophecy preachers and authors who believe that 1967 was a Jubilee year. What happened in 1967 was a huge event. It was the famous Six-Day War in Israel. That is what history calls it. Israel became a nation in May of 1948 but they were much smaller then. They did not have the Golan Heights or the West Bank, but more importantly, they did not possess Jerusalem. What is Israel without Jerusalem? During this famous Six-Day War,

Israel was attacked by several Arab nations. If you do some research you will find many miraculous things took place and Israel defeated her enemies and won the Golan Heights, the West Bank area, and Jerusalem. The war lasted just six days.

Next would be the Yom Kippur War in the early 70's where they would acquire more land, but reclaiming Jerusalem in 1967 was an EPIC event! Because of the strange and miraculous things that happened, and the acquiring of the holy city of Jerusalem, some think it was a Jubilee year. It certainly fits the description of a Jubilee. The city of Jerusalem went back to the original owner, the Jews. Again, I am not saying that we know anything for sure, but what if it was a Jubilee? Is there any way we can know? Well, I decided to go back 50 years and see if anything unusual happened concerning Israel in 1917. What I learned was shocking! In 1917, the Jews were still scattered. Jerusalem was inhabited by the Muslim Turks, who were a very fierce group of fighters. A British General named Allenby was ordered to force the Turks out and claim Jerusalem for Great Britain. What happens next is almost out of a children's fairytale but go research this yourself and see. What I am telling you actually happened. Printing was primitive in those days, as was the airplane. In fact, very few had ever seen an airplane. General Allenby came up with a plan. He decided to print some flyers and use airplanes to drop them over Jerusalem. The flyer said something like, "Get out of Jerusalem" and was signed Allenby. At least something like that written in Arabic. As I said, printing was primitive in those days. When the flyers arrived the name Allenby looked a lot like Allah in Arabic.

In fact it is said to have been written as Alla Bay, which means Son of God in Arabic. When the Turks looked up and saw airplanes in the sky, something they may have never seen before, and began to read the flyers, they read it as follows: "Get out of Jerusalem now!" signed Son of God. When General Allenby showed up days later with an army, they walked into Jerusalem and took it without firing one shot. What an amazing story! Now, does this have any characteristics of a Jubilee year?

Consider the Following Scenario

In 1917 on a Jubilee year, God gives Jerusalem to Great Britain, the Christian nation of the world at that time. Fifty years later on the 69th Jubilee, God gives Jerusalem back to those to whom it was promised, the Jews. In the next Jubilee, fifty years later in the fall of 2017, on God's 70th, and final Jubilee, Jerusalem goes back to God who is the original owner. Again, I am not saying that 2017 is the final 70th Jubilee. I am saying it could be. If 1917 and 1967 were Jubilee years, then 2017 would also be a Jubilee year. It is interesting, is it not? I am sure you have already figured out that there are not enough years from now to the year 2017 to fit in the Seven-year Tribulation. Here is one of the missing pieces of the puzzle that most prophecy preachers have missed. **The entire Tribulation is Daniel's 70th week and therefore is Old Testament.**

I believe the Church Age clock will stop at the rapture and the Old Testament clock will resume right where it left off to finish off the 4000 year period. I want to caution you about trying to set a date. We have looked at some very exciting scenarios here, but they are just some possibilities. The only thing we can be sure of is that the Lord is coming at the day appointed and no man knows the day or the hour. It is near impossible to figure out the calendar. It has been messed with. I cannot be sure that 1917 or 1967 were Jubilee years. God has not told us they were; I am just speculating. What I do know is that the next Jubilee will be the 70th Jubilee. Now that is very significant if I may say so. I do not know when the Lord is coming for us. I believe it is soon. I believe it may be very soon. That is all I am saying.

Joseph a Type of Christ

Chapter Nine

The Bible is filled with figures and types. Look at the following Scriptures.

✓ *Hebrews 9:24 For Christ is not entered into the holy places made with hands, which are the figures of the true; but into heaven itself, now to appear in the presence of God for us:*

✓*Hebrews 9:9 Which was a figure for the time then present, in which were offered both gifts and sacrifices, that could not make him that did the service perfect, as pertaining to the conscience;*

✓*Hebrews 8:4-5 For if he were on earth, he should not be a priest, seeing that there are priests that offer gifts according to the law: Who serve unto the example and shadow of heavenly things, as Moses was admonished of God when he was about to make the tabernacle: for, See, saith he, that thou make all things according to the pattern shewed to thee in the mount.*

✓ *Colossians 2:17 Which are a shadow of things to come; but the body is of Christ.*

There are some amazing similarities between Joseph and Christ, some figures or types if you will. We are not going to take a lot of time or space to list all the Scriptures. We just want to give you a rough outline. Let us just list them here for you. We think you will find these quite exciting.

1. Both Jesus and Joseph were beloved of their Father.
2. Joseph had a coat of many colors, a coat for which the soldiers gambled.
3. Joseph was sent to seek out his brothers and bring them bread. Hey, Jesus, the "bread of life" was sent to seek and to save that which was lost.
4. Joseph was rejected and despised of his brothers. Jesus, a man of sorrows, despised and rejected of men. (Isaiah 53) *He came unto his own, and his own received him not.* (John 1:11)
5. Joseph was thrown into a pit; Jesus went to the lower parts of the earth.
6. Joseph was sold into slavery. Jesus was sold for 30 pieces of silver.
7. Joseph and Jesus both spent time in Egypt.
8. Joseph and Jesus were both falsely accused.
9. Joseph and Jesus both suffered unjustly.
10. Joseph was sent to prison, Jesus to the cross and the tomb.
11. Joseph survived prison and sat on the right hand of the most-high Pharaoh. Jesus overcame the grave to sit at the right hand of the Most High God!
12. Joseph was given a Gentile bride. Jesus was also

given a Gentile Bride, the Church.

13. Joseph's brothers, the Jews, came into Egypt three times seeking bread. Remember, because of the famine, Jacob sent them to buy bread. Three times the Jews have entered the land of promise, first in the book of Exodus, second after the 70-year captivity, and the third time in 1948/1967.
14. Joseph's brothers came face to face with him but did not recognize him. Jesus came face to face with Israel but they did not recognize Him as the Messiah. The Jews for the most part, are still blinded.
15. Joseph revealed himself to his Jewish brothers after the third time they entered the land of Egypt, but ONLY after he ordered all the Gentiles out of the room. Remember, he ordered the Egyptians out, and then shocked his brothers when he said, *"I am Joseph, does my father yet live?"* Hey, Israel has entered the Promised Land three times now. Jesus is getting ready to reveal Himself to them, but ONLY after He orders all the Gentiles off the earth at the rapture. "I am Jesus whom thou persecutest..." Jesus said to Saul of Tarsus. It will not be long; we are going to be taken out of the way!

√

Joseph was given a Gentile bride. Jesus was also given a Gentile bride, the Church.

~Dan Goodwin

When Did the New Testament Age Begin?

Chapter Ten

January 2000 found a number of Christians wondering if this would be the year of Christ's return. Many were "packing up" spiritually speaking by expecting the rapture while others were "stocking up" for the Y2K crisis that never was. Some were under the impression Jesus would surely come after 2,000 years of the New Testament Age but as we will see, it was not the 2,000th year of the New Testament Age after all.

(Psalms 90:12) "*So teach us to number our days, that we may apply our hearts unto wisdom.*" If one were to attempt to number the days or years of the New Testament Age, would we start at the birth of Christ, His baptism or His death? When did the New Testament Age begin? We believe the New Testament Age began not at the birth of Christ, but rather at Calvary. Let us give you several reasons why we strongly believe this.

1. The Observance of the Sabbath

From the time of Moses, though the entire earthly life of Christ, the Sabbath was observed. Jesus, our example, always honored the Sabbath day, visited the synagogues, and observed the feast days. Does this sound like the New Testament Age to you? Not until after His death, burial, and resurrection did Christians gather on the first day of the week after the example of the Apostles. The Old Testament was spent laboring six days then resting on the Sabbath. Christ paid the sin debt at Calvary and we have already entered into His rest (Hebrews Chapter 4). Praise the Lord! Now for nearly 2,000 years, we gather on Sunday the Lord's Day and labor for Him the rest of the week because we are already eternally saved!

2. The Sacrifices

The Old Testament sacrifices were being offered throughout the earthly life of our Saviour. Christ even died on the Eve of Passover (Nisan 14), the same day the lambs were being slain. Does observing the Old Testament sacrifices sound like a New Testament doctrine to you? Christ became our sacrifice at Calvary thus ending the need to picture His death by the slaying of animals.

(Hebrews 10:10-12) "*By the which will we are sanctified through the offering of the body of Jesus Christ once for all. And every priest standeth daily ministering and offering oftentimes the same sacrifices, which can never take away sins: But this man, after he had offered one sacrifice for sins for ever, sat down on the right hand of God;*"

3. The Veil of the Temple

(Matthew 27:50-51) "*Jesus, when he had cried again with a loud voice, yielded up the ghost. And, behold, the veil of the temple was rent in twain from the top to the bottom; and the earth did quake, and the rocks rent;*" The veil in the temple was not rent in twain until after Jesus died. This veil was a barrier between God and man and could only be passed through by a High Priest. This veil was no longer needed because Jesus who became our sacrifice had just become our High Priest. At the very moment of His death, our Saviour cried out, "It is finished." He was speaking of three things, His physical life, the payment for sin, and the Old Testament Age. Would the New Testament Age have begun before the veil of the temple was torn from top to bottom? The answer is no.

Ephesians 2

11 Wherefore remember, that ye being in time past Gentiles in the flesh, who are called Uncircumcision by that which is called the Circumcision in the flesh made by hands;

12 That at that time ye were without Christ, being aliens from the commonwealth of Israel, and strangers from the covenants of promise, having no hope, and without God in the world:

13 But now in Christ Jesus ye who sometimes were far off are made nigh by the blood of Christ.

14 For he is our peace, who hath made both one, and hath broken down the middle wall of partition between us;

15 Having abolished in his flesh the enmity, even the law of commandments contained in ordinances; for to make in himself of twain one new man, so making peace;

16 And that he might reconcile both unto God in one body by the cross, having slain the enmity thereby:

17 And came and preached peace to you which were afar off, and to them that were nigh.

18 For through him we both have access by one Spirit unto the Father.

4. The Death of the Testator

(Hebrews 9:15-17) "*And for this cause he is the mediator of the new testament, that by means of death, for the redemption of the transgressions that were under the first testament, they which are called might receive the promise of eternal inheritance. For where a testament is, there must also of necessity be the death of the testator. For a testament is of force after men are dead: otherwise it is of no strength at all while the testator liveth.*" If a man were to record his last will and testament, an interesting thing takes place. A promise and certain conditions are made and are considered legal but not binding until a very important event takes place; the death of the testator. Christ is the Lamb slain from the foundation of the world. This was sealed in the foreknowledge of God and at the cross of Calvary the testator died for the sins of the world and the New Testament Age began.

See some definitions from Webster's 1828:

- TESTA'TOR, n. [L.] A man who makes and leaves a will or testament at death.
- TEST'AMENT, n. [L. testamentum, from testor, to make a will.]

1. A solemn authentic instrument in writing, by which a person declares his will as to the disposal of his estate and effects after his death. This is otherwise called a will. A testament, to be valid, must be made when the testator is of sound mind, and it must be subscribed, witnessed and published in such manner as the law prescribes.

A man in certain cases may make a valid will by words

only, and such will is called nuncupative.

2. The name of each general division of the canonical books of the sacred Scriptures; as the Old Testament; the New Testament. The name is equivalent to covenant, and in our use of it, we apply it to the books, which contain the old and new dispensations; that of Moses, and that of Jesus Christ.

5. The Old Testament Saints

(Ephesians 4:7-10) "*But unto every one of us is given grace according to the measure of the gift of Christ. Wherefore he saith, When he ascended up on high, he led captivity captive, and gave gifts unto men. (Now that he ascended, what is it but that he also descended first into the lower parts of the earth? He that descended is the same also that ascended up far above all heavens, that he might fill all things.)*" There are two examples in the Bible about saints who died and went to Paradise. One example is seen in Luke Chapter 16. Lazarus died and was "*carried by the angels into Abraham's bosom.*" Another time is the thief on the cross who trusted Jesus and was told by Christ; "*Today thou shalt be with me in paradise.*" (See Luke 23:43) Once the New Testament Age begins, every saint who dies is absent from the body and present with the Lord.

2 Corinthians 5:8

"We are confident, I say, and willing rather to be absent from the body, and to be present with the Lord."

6. Daniel's 69 weeks of prophecy

(Daniel 9:24-26) "*Seventy weeks are determined upon thy people and upon thy holy city, to finish the transgression, and to make an end of sins, and to make reconciliation for iniquity, and to bring in everlasting righteousness, and to seal up the vision and prophecy, and to anoint the most Holy. Know therefore and understand, that from the going forth of the commandment to restore and to build Jerusalem unto the Messiah the Prince shall be seven weeks, and threescore and two weeks: the street shall be built again, and the wall, even in troublous times. And after threescore and two weeks shall Messiah be cut off, but not for himself: and the people of the prince that shall come shall destroy the city and the sanctuary; and the end thereof shall be with a flood, and unto the end of the war desolations are determined."* Daniel's 69 weeks (483 years) were counting down from the time of Nehemiah until Christ the Messiah was cut off at Calvary. The ending of this prophetic countdown was not the birth of Christ but rather the death of Christ on the cross. After the New Testament Age ends with the rapture of the saints, Daniel's seventieth week (the Tribulation period) begins. This seventieth week completes the prophecy of Daniel chapter 9, and finishes off 4,000 years of the Old Testament. Bishop Ussher, from the 1600's, meant well when he put 4 B.C. for the date of the birth of Christ. He was simply trying to make the dates agree with the Roman solar calendar, but as we have said so often, nobody can understand prophecy as clearly as the generation living right before Christ comes for us! Listen to what Scofield said in his introduction to The Revelation; "Doubtless much which is designedly obscure to us will be clear to those for whom it was written as the time approaches."

Please note this chapter is titled, "*When did the New*

Testament Begin." It does not say "*When did the Church begin.*" Christ is the head of the church that was started during His earthly ministry when He called out the twelve. Christ is the Chief Cornerstone, the Apostles are the foundation and we are built on them. (Ephesians 2:20-22) *"And are built upon the foundation of the apostles and prophets, Jesus Christ himself being the chief corner stone; In whom all the building fitly framed together groweth unto an holy temple in the Lord: In whom ye also are builded together for an habitation of God through the Spirit."*

Just as in a normal physical birth, the head appears first followed by the rest of the body. Christ the head appeared first and the apostles and disciples followed. The rest of the church is built upon this foundation. A physical birth also includes a separation and cutting of the cord followed by the breath of life. Interestingly, after Christ paid the sin debt by dying for our sins He later ascended (separation) and the church breathed the breath of life (the Holy Spirit indwelling each believer) in the upper room and Pentecost. The church was clearly in existence several years before Calvary and the beginning of the New Testament Age.

"God did not put away the Old Testament laws; He fulfilled them."

— Dan Goodwin

What Year Is It Anyway?

Chapter Eleven

Unfortunately, the cycles of the sun and moon do not synchronize well (probably a result of the curse upon the world itself after the fall of Lucifer and man, or a result of the flood in Noah's day). A lunar year is 354 2/3rd days in length while a solar year is 365 1/4th days. Almost exactly in the middle is the prophetic year of 360 days. The number 360 is interesting for several reasons. There are 360 degrees in a perfect circle. There are 360 degrees on a compass. It is the sum of the angles of a four-sided object. It is the perfect number a perfect God uses to mark a prophetic year.

Let us give you some reasons to consider why we should not use the solar calendar in our prophetic studies.

1. **Consider who gave us the current calendar we use today.**

It was not Bible believing people, but rather the Romans with their belief in the sun god and many other heathen practices who gave us our calendar. It has been revised several times over the years, but the sun, not the moon, has been the premise.

2. **Consider the peoples who have used the sun (solstices, equinoxes, and eclipses, etc...) to measure their years and mark pagan and religious holidays.**

Egyptians, Babylonians, Persians, Romans, Druids, Celts, Inca, Mayan, Aztecs and others either worshiped the sun or the sun gods and marked their years by its position. None of these groups were ever accused of being Bible believing soul winners, to say the least.

3. **Consider that a prophetic year is 360 days not 365 and a quarter days and emphasis is on the moon not the sun.**

God uses the moon, not the sun to measure months and prophetic years. He speaks of 42 months as the last half of the Seven-year Tribulation, which is three and a half years. This is found in (Revelation 13:5) "*And there was given unto him a mouth speaking great things and blasphemies; and power was given unto him to continue forty and two months.*"

The entire Hebrew calendar is based on the moon. Each of their months started on the new moon. The Revelation speaks of the second half of the Tribulation as 1260 days. When you do the math, you find that is three and a half years of 360 days each. We believe at creation, the world was perfect and it took exactly 360 days for the earth to travel around the sun. Before the curse, the solar and lunar calendars were synchronized. A perfect God would not have a 365.24-day year, would He? After the curse, things changed and now it is out of order.

(Genesis 1:14-16) "*And God said, Let there be lights*

in the firmament of the heaven to divide the day from the night; and let them be for signs, and for seasons, and for days, and years: And let them be for lights in the firmament of the heaven to give light upon the earth: and it was so. And God made two great lights; the greater light to rule the day, and the lesser light to rule the night: he made the stars also."

God made the sun, moon, and the stars during the creative week. Besides giving light, they also are for determining signs and seasons. For example, Isaiah and Revelation, as well as the book of Joel, Matthew and others, all talk about the signs in the moon and sun concerning the last days. He speaks of the moon turning to blood before the second coming. God uses the sun and the moon for signs, but God uses the 360-day year for His prophetic calendar. The nation of Israel has always been under a lunar-based calendar, not the Roman calendar we use.

(Psalms 104:19) *"He appointed the moon for seasons: the sun knoweth his going down."*

(Psalms 89:37) *"It shall be established for ever as the moon, and as a faithful witness in heaven. Selah."* God uses the moon, not the sun, as an example of a faithful witness.

(Psalms 81:3) *"Blow up the trumpet in the new moon, in the time appointed, on our solemn feast day."* This is probably speaking of the Feast of trumpets, which begins on the first day of Tishri, which is their seventh month. Remember, their months always started on the new moon. All we are saying is that Israel always used a 360-day lunar, not solar calendar.

Take note of the following verses, which all speak of

1260 days making up a three and a half year period of time during the Tribulation. These are all in reference to a 360 day year.

(Revelation 11:3) "*And I will give power unto my two witnesses, and they shall prophesy a thousand two hundred and threescore days, clothed in sackcloth.*" Speaking of the first half (3 1/2 years) of the Tribulation.

(Revelation 12:6) "*And the woman fled into the wilderness, where she hath a place prepared of God, that they should feed her there a thousand two hundred and threescore days.*"

4. Our Gregorian (solar calendar) has a number of weaknesses.

It cannot be divided into equal halves or quarters; there are different numbers of days per month; and months or years may begin on any day of the week. Recent discoveries have also revealed that changes in the rotation of the earth (massive earthquakes) and changes in the earth's orbit around the sun affect the length of a day in hours and minutes. Since the sun is burning, it is constantly shrinking; causing the time it takes the earth to revolve around it to change slightly. Sound confusing? It is. Nobody will ever be able to prove exactly what year it is on God's prophetic calendar. God has ordained it that way. "*No man knows the day or the hour*!"

5. The solar calendar started at the wrong time!

As mentioned earlier, Bishop Ussher meant well, and we are sure he was acting on the information available to him at that time back in the 1600's. The Old Testament did not end until Christ died on Calvary when the veil of the temple was rent in two. We see this clearly in Daniel Chapter 9. Look at it here:

(Daniel 9:24-26) "*Seventy weeks are determined upon thy people and upon thy holy city, to finish the transgression, and to make an end of sins, and to make reconciliation for iniquity, and to bring in everlasting righteousness, and to seal up the vision and prophecy, and to anoint the most Holy. Know therefore and understand, that from the going forth of the commandment to restore and to build Jerusalem unto the Messiah the Prince shall be seven weeks, and threescore and two weeks: the street shall be built again, and the wall, even in troublous times. And after threescore and two weeks shall Messiah be cut off, but not for himself: and the people of the prince that shall come shall destroy the city and the sanctuary; and the end thereof shall be with a flood, and unto the end of the war desolations are determined.*"

Notice what we underlined in the verses above. The Bible clearly states that seventy weeks (490 years) are determined upon Israel. The 69th week, which is Old Testament, did not end at the birth of Christ, but at Calvary when Messiah was "cut off" as the text shows. My friend, as you can see in the passage above, Daniel's 70th week (Seven-year Tribulation) is also Old Testament! We also see this in (Hebrews 9:14-18) "*How much more shall the blood of Christ, who through the eternal Spirit offered himself without spot to God, purge your conscience from dead works to serve the living God? And for this cause he is the mediator of the new testament, that by means of death, for the redemption of the transgressions that were under the first testament, they which are called might receive the promise of eternal inheritance. For where a testament is, there must also of necessity be the death of the testator. For a testament is of force after men are dead: otherwise it is of no strength at all while the testator liveth. Whereupon neither the first testament was dedicated without blood."*

Any court of law would tell you that a will is not binding until the death of the person. Webster's 1828 Dictionary defines a Testator as: TESTA'TOR, n. [L.] A man who makes and leaves a will or testament at death.

The New Testament could not have begun until Christ went to the cross.

This is so simple yet everyone has missed it for centuries. We believe it is possible that this is part of the sealing up of the book as Daniel was told. We believe it is possible that this has been revealed in these last days to sound one last plea to the people of God to prepare for the Lord's soon return! Are you ready?

Apocalyptic Events in 2015

Chapter Twelve

Philippians 3:13 "Brethren, I count not myself to have apprehended: but this one thing I do, forgetting those things which are behind, and reaching forth unto those things which are before,"

2 Timothy 3:13 "But evil men and seducers shall wax worse and worse, deceiving, and being deceived."

Hebrews 10:25 "Not forsaking the assembling of ourselves together, as the manner of some is; but exhorting one another: and so much the more, as ye see the day approaching."

The year 2014 has come and gone. What a crazy year it turned out to be. It is now behind us. What transpired is now part of the annuals of history and cannot be changed. We have seen our country as well as the world slide deeper and deeper into lawlessness, immorality, hate and confusion. A darkness of deception is settling over America. We are seeing and hearing things we never imagined before. But, this progression happens to all nations that turn their backs on God.

" *Righteousness exalteth a nation: but sin is a reproach to any people*." (Proverbs 14:34)

I have to be honest, I do not see America turning back to God. I believe we are in the last of the last days. Everything is about to change. America has a much bigger role to play in end-time events than most people realize.

What does the future have in store for us? Let me share with you some important events I see on the horizon for 2015. I list them here in order of their occurrence. Some of these events have already occurred, some are yet to come or may have recently passed depending on when you are reading this chapter.

1. **March 20, 2015 is the 1st of Nisan on the Jewish calendar, 14 days before Passover. There was a solar eclipse on this day**.

Since several of the events I am going to mention have to do with signs in the heavens, let me give you a brief summary concerning them. The sun, the moon, and the stars have a purpose for their being. They are there to give us heat and light, and thank goodness for that. They are also there to measure days and months and years. However, they are also for signs.

"The heavens declare the glory of God; and the firmament sheweth his handywork. Day unto day uttereth speech, and night unto night sheweth knowledge. There is no speech nor language, where their voice is not heard." (Psalms 19:1-3)

Notice that the heavens speak to all regardless of tongue, language or nationality.

"And God said, Let there be lights in the firmament of the heaven to divide the day from the night; and let them be for

signs, and for seasons, and for days, and years:" (Genesis 1:14)

These "*lights*" are the sun, the moon, and the stars. They are for giving light and for dividing night from day. They are also for signs and seasons.

(Joel 2:30-31) "And I will shew wonders in the heavens and in the earth, blood, and fire, and pillars of smoke. The sun shall be turned into darkness, and the moon into blood, before the great and the terrible day of the LORD come."

"And I will shew wonders in heaven above, and signs in the earth beneath; blood, and fire, and vapour of smoke: The sun shall be turned into darkness, and the moon into blood, ***before*** *that great and notable day of the Lord come:" (Acts 2:19-20)*

"And there shall be signs in the sun, and in the moon, and in the stars; and upon the earth distress of nations, with perplexity; the sea and the waves roaring;" (Luke 21:25)

2. **A blood red moon occurred on Feast of Passover, April 4th, 2015 which is Nisan 14 on the Jewish calendar.**

A blood moon is a total lunar eclipse. There were two of these is 2014 on Feast of Passover and Feast of Tabernacles, and the final two (Making this a tetrad) are in 2015 starting on Feast of Passover on April 4th and ending on Feast of Tabernacles. This is the 8th Tetrad to occur on the Jewish Feast days in the last 2000 years. There will not be another of these tetrads on the Biblical Feast days for several centuries. A tetrad is a scientific term that means four. To an astronomer, a tetrad means four consecutive full lunar eclipses in a two year period. There have been several dozen tetrads in the last 2000 years, but this is only the 8th time since the New Testament began that they have been on the 1st and last Biblical feast days of Passover and Tabernacles. (See chapter 17 in my book GOD'S FINAL JUBILEE for an in depth study of the blood red moons.)

3. **September 13th, 2015 is the Biblical release date (Shemitah) for the Sabbatical year.**

In other words, if 2015 is a Sabbatical year, then 9-13-15 is the date that all debt is forgiven and all slaves are set free if you lived in Israel in Bible days. If it is a Sabbatical year, as most Jews claim, it would also be the 49th year of the Sabbatical cycle which means it is also a JUBILEE year! Since some of you may get a little fuzzy here, let me give you just a brief summary.

There are three main Sabbaths in the Bible that the Jews had to be concerned with:

a. Seventh day Sabbath. This is a Saturday. Most of us understand this one.

b. Seventh year Sabbath. Also referred to as the sabbatical year or cycle. This is the one referred to in the book, THE HARBINGER. On the Sabbatical year, the Jews were not to plant a crop in their fields. At the end of this seventh year all debt was forgiven and all slaves were set free. (Deuteronomy 15)

c. Seven Sabbatical cycles (49 years) is a high Sabbath called the Jubilee. All property goes back to the original owner on the Jubilee (See Leviticus 25)

Now, if the Jews are right and this is in fact a Sabbatical year, then 9-13-15 is the Biblical release date, the Shemitah. In other words, it is the exact day that the slaves and debt would be released in Israel. It happens just before sundown. At sundown is Rosh Hashanah and the start of a new year. It is the exact same day the stock market crashed both in 2001 and 2008. The date on the Biblical calendar was/is Elul 29. Could this be significant? I believe it would be very foolish to just brush this away as not important. By the way, 9-13-15 is a Sunday and the stock market will be closed. However, Friday before just happens to be 9-11-15. Well, do I have your attention now?

4. 9-13-15 happens to be another solar eclipse.

This is the second solar eclipse of the year. It occurs on the same day as the Sabbatical release date we just discussed.

5. Feast of Trumpets occurs at sundown on 9-13-15.

The Jews call it Rosh Hashanah, meaning "Head of the year." Many folks will be looking for the rapture on this day. Feast of Trumpets is certainly prophetic of the rapture. It takes place each year on the new moon of the month Tishri. It is the first of the three fall feasts. Jesus fulfilled the first four feasts right to the day. These last three are prophetic of the last days and have yet to be fulfilled.

6. **On 9-28-15, which is the Feast of Tabernacles, the second blood red moon of this year takes place.**

Feast of Tabernacles is the 7th feast of the 7th month of the Jewish calendar. This is the 4th and final blood red moon of the tetrad.

7. **9-28-15 is not only a blood red moon, but also a super moon.**

A Super Moon is a full moon that takes place as the moon is at its closest point to the earth in its orbit. Therefore, it is bigger when viewed. But there is something else interesting about this. Of the four blood red moons of the tetrad of 2014/2015, this is the only one that will actually be visible in the skies over Jerusalem! Is that interesting? So what we have on this day over the city of Jerusalem is a full lunar eclipse that is referred to as a blood moon, during the rare occurrence of a Super Moon. And it happens to be the 4th blood moon of the tetrad on the 7th Jewish Feast during the 7th month of the Jewish calendar.

These seven points are just the things we know about and are sure about. Now what they mean to us in a prophetic light is for each of us to decide for himself. Whether the Lord comes back this year or not, these are rare and amazing things that are taking place. Besides what I just gave you, consider these events happening in America and across the globe:

-America's debt is now over 18 trillion and nobody seems concerned.
-Sodomy and other immorality has become a normal and accepted lifestyle.
-Israel surrounded by more dangerous enemies than ever before.
-Russia showing signs of moving south.
-The one world order can be clearly seen.
-The one world religion and its leader is here.
-Iran is very close to weapons of mass destruction.
-The churches of the world fit the description of the "Lukewarm" church in Revelation 3.
-The appearance of "Strong delusion" already among us.
-Terrorism rampant around the world.

Folks, be ready. Everything is about to change! The Antichrist is alive and ready somewhere on the earth. The one world order is here and awaiting the time to move. Man is nearly ready to receive the false Gospel of the False Prophet. Right here in America we are one suitcase nuke or one national calamity away from being placed under Martial Law. This is not the time to be backslidden. This is no time to be living a life of sin. My friend, this is a time to be vigilant! This is a time to be busy about God's business. We must do all we can to warn our friends and neighbors and lead the lost to Jesus. I leave you with the admonition from the following Scripture. Keep looking unto Jesus!

"Looking unto Jesus the author and finisher of our faith; who for the joy that was set before him endured the cross, despising the shame, and is set down at the right hand of the throne of God." (Hebrews 12:2)

"I believe we are near the end: I believe we are on the final lap of this age. The finish line is just around the next bend. It is not time to be lazy: it is not time to lag behind. It is time to pull out all the stops and run harder and faster than we ever have before!"

~Dan Goodwin

Time is Running Out

Chapter Thirteen

Everything is about to change. Time is running out. The trumpet is getting ready to sound in Heaven and all the believers will be snatched from off the earth to meet the Lord in the clouds of Glory. Very soon, Jesus is coming in what is known as the rapture. Once the sand in the hourglass has run out, it will be too late for those who do not know the Lord. Friend, time is short; the trumpet IS getting ready to sound. Jesus IS getting ready to come for the church. We are at the end of all things! If you are left behind, you will have to live through the worst time in the history of the world. We call it the Seven-year Tribulation. Look what the Bible says about this terrible time:

Matthew 24:21 For then shall be great tribulation, such as was not since the beginning of the world to this time, no, nor ever shall be.

Friend, look at just some of the horror that will be poured out upon the earth during the Tribulation:

Revelation 6:8 And I looked, and behold a pale horse: and his name that sat on him was Death, and Hell followed with him. And power was given unto them over the fourth part of the earth, to kill with sword, and with hunger, and with death, and with the beasts of the earth.

Revelation 6:16 And said to the mountains and rocks, Fall

on us, and hide us from the face of him that sitteth on the throne, and from the wrath of the Lamb:

Revelation 6:17 For the great day of his wrath is come; and who shall be able to stand?

Revelation 9:1-2 And the fifth angel sounded, and I saw a star fall from heaven unto the earth: and to him was given the key of the bottomless pit. And he opened the bottomless pit; and there arose a smoke out of the pit, as the smoke of a great furnace; and the sun and the air were darkened by reason of the smoke of the pit.

Revelation 9:5-6 And to them it was given that they should not kill them, but that they should be tormented five months: and their torment was as the torment of a scorpion, when he striketh a man. And in those days shall men seek death, and shall not find it; and shall desire to die, and death shall flee from them.

Friend, imagine a world without Christians. Imagine all the Bible believing churches are empty. Worse yet, imagine living in a world without God for seven years. The Tribulation is a time of wrath from God upon Satan and upon those who reject the Lord Jesus Christ and is literally getting ready to happen. The hour is later than you think. Friend, are you prepared to meet the Lord? Are you ready for the trumpet to sound? Are you "Rapture ready?"

What you need to be Rapture ready:

1. **You must be a saved born again child of God to be "Rapture ready."**

To be saved you first need to see yourself as God sees you, a sinner under the condemnation of a holy God.

Romans 3:10 As it is written, There is none righteous, no, not one.

Romans 3:23 For all have sinned, and come short of the glory of God;

Romans 6:23 For the wages of sin is death; but the gift of God is eternal life through Jesus Christ our Lord.

The sinner has death and hell as his payment for sin, but God's gift is salvation when we trust in the Lord Jesus Christ and his blood that was shed for our sin on the cross of Calvary

Romans 6:23 For the wages of sin is death; but the gift of God is eternal life through Jesus Christ our Lord.

Romans 10:9-13 That if thou shalt confess with thy mouth the Lord Jesus, and shalt believe in thine heart that God hath raised him from the dead, thou shalt be saved. For with the heart man believeth unto righteousness; and with the mouth confession is made unto salvation. For the scripture saith, Whosoever believeth on him shall not be ashamed. For there is no difference between the Jew and the Greek: for the same Lord over all is rich unto all that call upon him. For whosoever shall call upon the name of the Lord shall be saved.

Friend, simply bow your head and admit to God that you are a sinner on your way to an eternity in hell. Repent of your unbelief and place your trust in the Lord Jesus Christ to wash away your sins and save you from the penalty of your sin. Put your complete faith and trust in Christ and be saved, believing that Jesus is the virgin born Son of God who died, was buried, and rose from the grave to pay your sin debt.

John 3:16 For God so loved the world, that he gave his only begotten Son, that whosoever believeth in him should not perish, but have everlasting life.

2. **To be "Rapture ready" you need to be right with the Lord, living a life that is pleasing to God according to the Bible.**

1 Peter 1:16 Because it is written, Be ye holy; for I am holy.
Friend, the Lord is returning very soon. Are you going to be ashamed of some things in your life when He returns? Why not get your life in order now while there is still time. Will you be ashamed when you meet the Lord and look into His eyes?

3. **To be "Rapture ready" you need to be watching for the Lord's return.**

Matthew 24:42 Watch therefore: for ye know not what hour your Lord doth come.

Friend, we are to be watching and expecting the soon return of the Lord.

Luke 12:37 Blessed are those servants, whom the lord when he cometh shall find watching: verily I say unto you, that he shall gird himself, and make them to sit down to meat, and will come forth and serve them.

Look at the admonition the Lord gives to those whom He finds watching when He comes. Wouldn't you like to receive that blessing from the Lord?

Friend, are you "Rapture ready?" Are you saved? Are you living a life that is pleasing to the Lord? Are you watching for the return of the Lord? He is coming for us very soon. I pray that you are ready.

*****This is an excerpt from a gospel tract that is available at www.godsfinaljubilee.com.**

✓

"The same preachers who criticize prophecy, do not seem to have a problem setting a date to go golfing in the "FUTURE"!

— Dan Goodwin

Last Words for These Last Days

Chapter 14

Some may be asking, "Why study prophecy?" Well, since the Bible is literally filled with prophetic truths, it would be hard to study the Bible without learning prophetic truths. The Bible admonishes us to know the future. Consider the following passages of Scripture:

Isaiah 45:11 "*Thus saith the LORD, the Holy One of Israel, and his Maker, Ask me of things to come concerning my sons, and concerning the work of my hands command ye me.*"

Revelation 1:1 "*The Revelation of Jesus Christ, which God gave unto him, to shew unto his servants things which must shortly come to pass; and he sent and signified it by his angel unto his servant John:*"

Almost the entire book of Daniel and most of the Revelation as well as parts of many other books of the Bible are prophetic. God wants us to be interested in the future. The truth is the Bible is a futuristic book. Even though many will say they are not concerned with future events, the opposite is true. Do you know that all of us are actually living for the future? Let us prove it to you. They tell us there are around six billion people on the earth today, and nearly every one of them, including you and me, are living for the future. Most of you will check the weather this evening to see what you need to wear tomorrow. In fact, many will look at not only the weather for tomorrow, but also the weather for the next ten days. Now, we can even get weather by the hour on our computers and weather alerts on our cell phones concerning possible bad weather to come. Are you still not convinced we are a generation living for the future? Young people are looking forward to getting to High School. High School kids cannot wait to graduate and either get out of school or go on to college. College folks look forward to getting their career started. Young adults look forward to marriage. Couples look forward to children. People at their jobs look forward to a promotion. Hey, how about the following common statements we all use: "I can't wait for the weekend, payday, or Friday!" "I can hardly wait for my income tax return." "I can hardly wait for my vacation to get here." We look forward to getting a house, having grandchildren, retirement, and on and on we could go. Have we made our point? All of us are in reality, living for the future!

Basically, prophecy is the future. Prophecy is history pre-written. The same "scoffers" who criticize prophecy, do not have a problem saving money for the future, planning for a vacation in the future, or setting a date to go golfing in THE FUTURE!

The book you are holding in your hands was not written to scare anyone. This book was written to sound an alarm to the people of God. Jesus is coming, and He is coming soon! We do not know the exact date of His coming, nor can we be sure what year He is coming, but we believe it will be soon. At the end of each age, God has a few men who sound the horn for the next generation. Noah sounded the horn before the floods came. Jeremiah and Ezekiel sounded the horn concerning the seventy-year captivity to come. Daniel sounded the horn at the end of the seventy-years and Ezra and Nehemiah led in the rebuilding of the city. John the Baptist sounded the horn for the coming of Christ. God will have two witnesses, Elijah and Moses sounding the horn right before the Jews trust the Messiah during the Tribulation. After considering all this, do you think God would end the New Testament Age without raising up some men to sound the horn to warn the people of the next event to come? Not on your life! We believe God will raise up men to sound the horn and warn the people of His soon coming! We believe God could use the truths in this book to stir preachers across our land to once again not only look for, but to once again hope for the soon return of Christ.

The most important and exciting part of a race is the finish. When a runner gets to the last lap he seems to find strength within him to push a little harder and to give one final effort to win. My friend, we believe we are near the end. We believe we could be on the final lap of this age. The finish line may be just ahead. It is not time for a pit stop! It is not time to take a vacation. It is time to pull out all the stops and run harder and faster than we ever have before! Brethren, let us go out with a bang! Let us not be the generation that quit on the last mile, let us be the generation that crossed that finish line in a blaze of glory! Let us do it for souls, let us do it for our churches, let us do it for God!

He which testifieth these things saith, Surely I come quickly. Amen. Even so, come, Lord Jesus.

~Revelation 22:20

MORE FROM GOODWIN PUBLICATIONS

www.godsfinaljubilee.com

Biblical Forgiveness

God's Final Jubilee

Revelation

God's Final Jubilee DVD Set

Time is Running Out Gospel Tract

Prophecy Conferences

Evangelist Dan Goodwin travels extensively, speaking in Prophecy Meetings and Bible Conferences across the nation. He has authored several books and study guides. Contact him to schedule a meeting or to get information on his books.

PROPHECY CONFERENCE TOPICS

* Are we the last generation
* Signs of the times
* What year is it anyway
* The seven feasts: God's Prophetic Calendar
* A wedding made in Heaven
* Solid proof of a pre-tribulation rapture
* God's final Jubilee
* The blood red moons
* The seven feasts and the Christian life
* The seven sealed book
* A 7000 year prophetic view
* Prophetic figures and types
* 2520

Dan Goodwin
117 E. 18th St. #165
Owensboro, KY 42303
270-363-6336
www.godsfinaljubilee.com